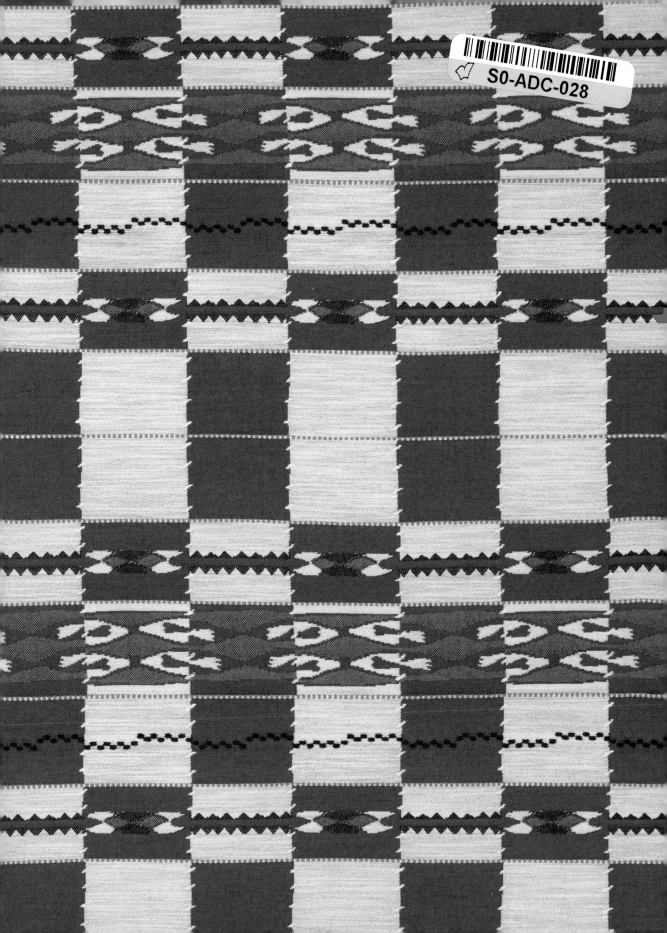

# Kit Kemp
# DESIGN SECRETS

To all who have suffered in 2020, especially our good
friends in the world of hospitality.

# Kit Kemp
# DESIGN SECRETS

Photography by Simon Brown

Hardie Grant

BOOKS

# CONTENTS

# WHAT DO I WANT FROM AN INTERIOR?

**Time to let go of conformity and be true to myself – for my interiors to comfortably say 'This is me' and to enjoy that experience. I may want to be tidier, more beautiful and immaculate, but life isn't like that – it is forever evolving. So too, should my interiors be open to change, to new colours and ideas, and to move on organically.**

My living space acts like a mirror to my thoughts and feelings. It should restore and rejuvenate and be the central hub of joy and activity.

It is fun to think creatively at home. Get everyone involved – they will love it more and feel proud to have taken part. *Design Secrets* is about giving a simple nudge to get going. Just one little seed of an idea can create a whole new way of looking at interiors. If this book can give you confidence, inspire fresh thoughts or provide a new and different viewpoint, then I have succeeded.

I believe the best rooms never want us to leave. There is a certain something that captures the imagination and stays with us forever.

I can look back on rooms that feel a part of me and are important in my life. They are uplifting and overwhelmingly nostalgic, very precious and timeless. There are the treasures, like a weathervane of a fox and an old wooden marquetry sewing box filled with photographs, that follow me around; it would not be home without them. I hope to create rooms that welcome and embrace all the senses.

Let's keep the valuable, re-evaluate the unnecessary, and if you can't bear to get rid of something, let's celebrate the experience and make a collection. It needn't be silver or gold. It can be a collection of buttons, shoe buckles or old keys. Or you never know, perky Perspex and a patchwork lampshade might give the perfect finishing touch. They will certainly create a talking point.

I hope *Design Secrets* helps to reappraise your surroundings in an artistic and colourful way – and remember, the thoughtfulness and character of a lovingly made object is worth a million times more than an accessory that has no meaning or soul.

*Opposite: Kit Kemp at home*

OUT
AND
ABOUT

# A DAY IN THE STUDIO

On a leafy street in South Kensington, in London, you will find our design studio. Every day is different: we could be working on a new scheme for a house or hotel, meeting with artists and designers or visiting a new gallery or exhibition for inspiration.

## Sourcing

One of the most important aspects of our work is sourcing. We are always seeking new and interesting pieces for the designs we are working on. Every week, we are regularly visited by designers, artists, artisans and craftspeople. Together we look over their new collections, giving them the opportunity to tell us a bit about the inspiration behind them.

## Scheming

Scheming is an equally important part of our day. We are continuously reinventing interiors and developing new schemes. On Wednesday mornings, we often meet to discuss our latest plans and ideas. It is like a show-and-tell, where all the team takes part, contributing their revelations of the week or a piece of furniture or fabric that has inspired them. It is one of my favourite times. I love to see and hear their enthusiasm – it has become a reason for lots of laughter and a forum for bright ideas to emerge.

When creating a new room scheme, we are guided by our love of fabric. We often start with a large-scale pattern as the main design, and then pick out aspects of this to build the scheme's story. Finding a main fabric that you love will provide guidance for the rest of the room and will establish its 'rhythm'. Large-scale, multicoloured fabrics might be scary, but they provide a focal point – acting like a 'canvas' – for a room. If in doubt, use plain colours and fabrics on the perimeter of the room and add the pattern and detail to the central pieces, such as on the sofa cushions or a statement chair.

Once your key fabric has been identified, it is possible to mix different patterns of varying sizes. Use one fabric with a large-scale pattern, one medium-scale and one small-scale – together, these pieces of the puzzle will come together to create a single beautiful creation.

After a day of meetings, scheming and sourcing, we will often get together in the garden to hear about each other's projects over a cup of tea.

How to make your house fabulously
different, and as unique as you are

# CREATING CHARACTER

# A SNEAK PEAK

**We invite you to take a sneak peek at a recent residential renovation in London.**

This drawing room (above and opposite) is a bright and airy space which stretches from the front to the back of the house. I have used my oversized 'One Way' fabric for Christopher Farr Cloth on one of the walls and on the curtains surrounding the arched windows. Playing with different scales of pattern in a room makes you look twice.

Between the two arched windows is an 18th-century Spanish chest (left). A strong piece of furniture is grounding in such a vibrant space.

I completely reconfigured the ground floor to create a new entrance hall (below) which is dramatically lined in my 'Mythical Lands' wallpaper. A space like this can be easily forgotten – here, the large repeat fills the space from floor to ceiling, creating dramatic impact and immediately drawing a visitor into the interior.

In the living room (overleaf), vignettes of handmade, organic pieces eclectically arranged together around the room lend the feeling of a series of still-life paintings set within a still life painting.

Adjoining the kitchen, I created a light and airy dining space (above and left). At the head of the table, one of my 'Kit's Wing' armchairs and the curtain pelmets are covered in a Raoul Textiles fabric to help unify the room's design scheme. Tord Boontje's Ivy Chandelier for Porta Romana creates lovely shadow lines across the ceiling.

In the guest bedroom (above), the headboard, curtains and pillows are in my 'Hedgerow' design, paired with a bedspread in Blithfield's 'Anoushka' fabric. The armchair covered in my 'Lost and Found' fabric lends gravitas to the room, while additional texture, such as Katherine Cuthbert flower paintings on the wall and the antique rattan-backed settee, helps the scheme to strike a harmonious whole.

# EXQUISITE EMBROIDERY

**I have always cherished intricately embroidered fabrics, from tapestries and rugs to embellished felts – I love the way textiles so often tell a story in their exquisite craftsmanship.**

Layering textures always helps to make rooms come alive, especially when working with beautifully hand-embroidered textiles like the ones I have used throughout The Whitby Suite at

The Whitby Hotel in New York (above and opposite).

Embroidery, as a wonderful art form; it makes a room feel more unique and handcrafted.

Pippa Caley is an artisan I love to collaborate with regularly – her work is intricate and yet appears so simple, with a wonderful raw finish. She sketches directly onto the fabric with her sewing machine, over which she then collages and embroiders to create interesting fabrics. This layering techniques makes a fabric feel so much more personal.

I sent Pippa the fabric pattern of the Chesterfield sofa in The Whitby Suite, onto which she embroidered these beautifully delicate floral designs (far left).

At the opposite end of the room (bottom), another sofa covered in my fabric 'Bookends', designed for Christopher Farr Cloth, is layered with Pippa's hand-embroidered cushions, which lift the indigo colourway with their subtle but eye-catching flashes of red embroidered motifs. It is this close attention to such tactile details that makes people feel immediately welcome, and indeed, never want to leave a room.

Contemporary embroidery plays with all sorts of abstract stitches, knots and purls, and while it can look both masculine and feminine, it should not be too dainty. Embroidery, like my 'Bookend' fabric, can lend bold strength and movement to any design scheme.

Embroidered textiles work well for providing a focus point in a room. In the master bedroom (opposite and above), an exquisitely hand-embroidered headboard by Natasha Hulse adds drama with its vibrant colours and textures.

Natasha originally studied Fashion Design at Chelsea College of Arts, and this is one of the first headboards she designed for me. Its magnificent 'Tree of Life' design, with little beads intricately sewn onto the leaves, appliqué butterflies and three-dimensional centres of the flowers, feels like a special piece of couture, lending a magical, one-off personal touch to the room. You can almost imagine her hands working over the fabric, bringing it to life.

# DADO DEVIANTS

Traditionally, dado rails were installed to prevent chair backs from damaging the walls, but now they are often removed from rooms because they are considered outdated. However, I see a dado rail as an opportunity to combine different fabrics and materials. It can be a lot of fun combining different textures such as wallpaper, fabric, paint and wooden panelling in the one scheme.

The best part of working with a dado rail is that it can be easily created with just a simple strip of shaped wood, a wide trimming or even a strip of wallpaper.

In this Shepherd's Hut, we created a painted dado rail to divide the mural. Above it is a mythical landscape with rolling hills and pear trees, while below it, vivid red cartouches have been decorated with joyful jugs of flowers and leaping horses.

In the Araminta Room at The Whitby Hotel (right), I used my 'Mythical Land' design above the dado rail, paired with a contrasting striped fabric skirt of navy and electric blues below.

In London's Covent Garden Hotel (bottom right), I kept things simple by using Soane's tiny 'Coral' print wallpaper above a fresh white dado rail and painted Farrow & Ball's 'Shaded White' below. These colours were picked out from the Jim Thompson fabric used on the headboard.

In a reverse effect, (bottom left), Molly Mahon's geometric 'Luna' fabric is used below the dado rail, while a plain fabric has been used to line the wall above.

In London's Charlotte Street Hotel, a spring-green wallpaper by Brain Yates lines the walls above the dado rail, with Little Green's 'Old Paper' paint below. These two contrasting colours beautifully enhance the hues of the headboard and curtain fabrics, where I have used a green and pink Soane 'Tendril Vine' printed linen.

I love to rethink traditional designs with a contemporary twist. Dado rails are the perfect opportunity to settle the debate about which fabric, paint or wallpaper to use in your room – use them all!

HERE ARE MY TOP TIPS FOR

# DADO RAILS

1. Make sure the dado doesn't protrude any more than 5 mm (¼ in) from the wall.

2. The optimal height for a dado should be around 1–1.2 m (3–4 ft) from the floor – the general rule is that the higher the ceiling, the higher the position of the dado.

3. Always have more space above the dado rail than below.

4. Use a combination of plains and patterns – if you are worried about using a very bold wallpaper in a room, use it above the dado and calm it down with a plain paint or fabric finish below. This works particularly well for hallways and staircases.

5. Paint the dado rail in the same colour as your skirting and cornicing to create a seamless finish. The area between the dado and skirting can be a complementary colour tone.

# CREATING A COLLECTION

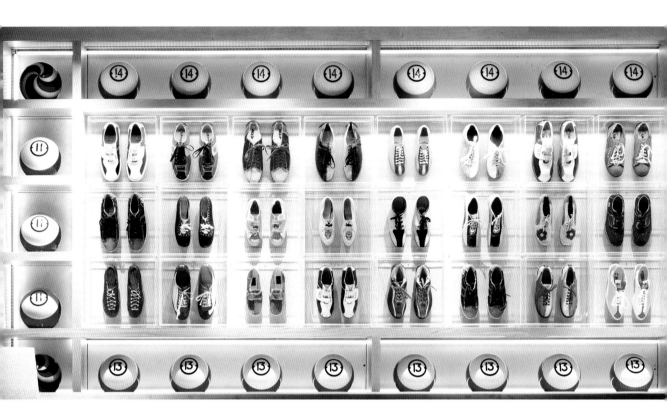

Collections of quirky objects, such as antique plates, unusual figurines or colourful ceramic pots, grouped together and cleverly framed, can suddenly take on a whole new meaning and become interesting artworks in their own right.

As you step into the Croc Bowling Alley at Ham Yard Hotel in London (above), you are greeted by a collection of 70 bowling shoes sourced on eBay over a year. The collection is framed by colourful bowling balls which makes these simple objects feel like an art installation.

A collection of meat platters, also found on eBay, line the walls of The Orangery at The Whitby Hotel (above). These are the wonderful large dishes that we associate with grandfather carving the Sunday roast. Set on a black felt background and encased in Perspex, they are elevated to works of art, beautifully offset against walls lined with my 'Travelling Light' design.

The Soho Hotel in London, was once the site of a car park (parking lot). In homage to the hotel's past life, a collection of old oil cans, containers and Dinky Toys makes a playful automobile montage in the Refuel Bar & Restaurant.

At Crosby Street Hotel, in New York (above), a
collection of vintage telephones mounted on the
wall and artfully lit become a witty focal point in
the restaurant.

A collection doesn't need to be created with rare collectibles or exquisite antiques – it can also be achieved with simple everyday objects. One of the collections I am most proud of is the installation of baskets hanging above The Whitby Bar (above). There are 52 in total, each basket originating from different areas of England, Scotland, Wales and Ireland, and although humble, everyday objects in themselves, when displayed together they become an eye-catching and impressive feature in this bustling Manhattan bar.

Often a single object on its own doesn't have much impact, but when displayed as part of a collection, it can be transformed into the most interesting feature in a room.

I encourage you to be bold, to think outside the box and enjoy the process of making art installations with your own collections.

# PILLOW TALK

Never underestimate the power of the cushion.
They are key for adding that little extra contrast,
pattern, texture and softness to a space, as well
as providing a tool for tying a scheme together
and creating balance within a room.

We regularly work with the charitable social enterprise Fine Cell Work, which was founded over 20 years ago by Lady Anne Tree with the aim of helping prisoners to develop new skills, earn money and acquire the self-belief to stop offending.

Our 'Heart of Oak' (top) and 'Rain Shadow' (bottom right) cushion designs, featuring a combination of French knots, stem and chain stitches on either a thick British boiled wool or fine linen, reflect my love of colour and embroidery. Only a handful of Fine Cell Work's stitchers have the necessary skills, so production is in small, limited batches, making them all the more covetable.

A wonderful way to make a
cushion your own is to combine
different fabrics and textures.
In this bedroom (above), the
headboard is covered in a
bespoke colourway of Baker
& Gray's hand-embroidered

'Monkey in a Fig Tree' fabric,
which we paired with matching
bed cushions to give the
scheme a personalised and
unique feel.

Here, a 'Wee Beasties Birds' cushion, from my embroidered collection with Chelsea Textiles, creates an interesting juxtaposition positioned on this one-off Brutalist chair. It is brave and surprises the eye.

# A RAY OF LIGHT

**As the sun is such a prominent feature in our lives, I wanted to share a little trick to make your interiors look more luminous.**

I am all about natural materials and creating a relaxed, comfortable atmosphere, but sometimes 'a touch of gold' can bring a ray of light that adds warmth and luminosity to a space.

In this mews house in London (above), I added golden touches by putting old paintings in gilt frames and hanging gilded works of art by Joe Tilson and Katherine Cuthbert on the living room walls (opposite, top right, bottom left and right). These give warmth to the scheme, creating an interesting contrast against the white linen walling.

A large cushion with pineapple embroidery by Fine Cell Work (opposite, top left) contrasts wonderfully with my green 'Criss Cross' fabric on the armchair.

In the Drawing Room of The Whitby Hotel (above), an antique gilded sunbeam mirror illuminates the room, providing the focal point for the space. It draws the eye through the scheme of fabric walling by Casamance and sofas upholstered in my 'Friendly Flowers' hand-embroidered fabric.

The fairy-tale combination of the sun paired with the unicorn console tables sitting either side of the fireplace looks magical, creating a place for guests to dream momentarily.

In The Whitby Hotel's Araminta Room, I assembled a small collection of golden 'sunburst' wall lights (above and right) – they give the impression of several cheerful suns put together, which adds a ray of light, and act like a window in this windowless room.

We designed and made this massive, golden, three-tier chandelier for The Orangery at The Whitby Hotel (above and left). Once hung, I added 1970s metal parrots to set a fun and glamorous mood – I love their intricate details, from the blue glass eyes to each little engraved feather. Unexpected ideas like this add a joyful feeling and make all the difference to a room.

Gilded frames on mirrors (above) or paintings work very well against almost all walling colours: for example, they warm up a white wall, make a terracotta wall feel lighter, and add contrast on a blue wall.

# PERKY PERSPEX

**I am known for my love of a myriad of materials and textures, and one unexpected material I use throughout my interiors is Perspex.**

Perspex is the household brand name for an acrylic sheet, first manufactured in 1933. The word Perspex is derived from the Latin word for 'see-through' – although hard and rigid, it can be bent into any shape, and is available in opaque and transparent options which can be matched to any colour.

Perspex adds a contemporary edge when used to display antique fabrics or a collection of objects such as these plates by Robina Jack (above), which share a wonderful synergy with the armchair placed below them, upholstered in my whimsical 'Moondog' design for Chelsea Textiles embroidered onto felt.

In Crosby Street Hotel's lobby (above), we have used Perspex to display a collection of ceramics by artist Daniel Reynolds within the coffee table. On the wall (right), we have used Perspex to frame a three-dimensional artwork by Jack Milroy. Perspex is a great material for creating deep box frames because it provides excellent clarity while being less heavy and expensive than glass. It also has a high shock resistance, making it less susceptible to damage.

You will find various collections displayed in Perspex, from a pair of pretty Gucci shoes set on Astroturf in the Drawing Room at Number Sixteen, in London, and framed felt toys, to the antique platter collection in The Whitby Bar & Restaurant (above). We also framed hand-painted plates (right) as part of an installation for my Bergdorf Goodman pop-up in New York.

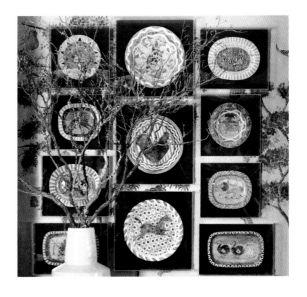

Museums and art galleries across the globe use Perspex to display their treasures because the advanced UV-grade option protects delicate artworks and fabrics. At Ham Yard Restaurant (left), we have framed antique Indian textiles to create low room dividers between dining tables. This adds privacy and structure within the space, while incorporating textural and visual interest. I love the contrast of framing this decorative Suzani in such a contemporary finish.

Our Rocket Lamp design (bottom left and right) brings an injection of colour to any scheme. Made entirely from Perspex and set on a wooden base, these fun geometric lamp bases exude a sculptural quality that creates great impact in any setting.

# A LOVE OF BOOKS

**Despite living in this digital age of iPads and Kindles, nothing compares to the romance of flicking through real pages, and absorbing the soothing, familiar smell of an old book.**

My very favourite rooms are always libraries, where books look so comforting upon the walls, instantly making a room feel cosy and ageless.

In the Reading Room at The Whitby Hotel (above and left), a curated collection of books on backlit shelves spans the entire wall. It is a dramatic way of accommodating decorative objects, which are stylishly arranged among the books.

I often hang paintings in front of bookcases (opposite) so the books themselves become a backdrop to the artworks, adding further depth to a room.

Placing antique mirror behind the bookshelves creates the illusion of more depth and space in a smaller room such as this small study (above). Walls lined with books (opposite, top) lend a further dimension of colour and texture to this inviting space.

At London's Knightsbridge Hotel – an old building full of character and architectural mouldings – a simple yet traditional bookcase showcasing old books and art sits behind an illuminated contemporary ladder to create an interesting contrast (opposite, bottom).

# A BEADY EYE –
# USING BEADS IN DESIGN

**When I'm designing a space, I love to use unusual materials and textures that add an extra layer of detail.**

The humble bead has been used for thousands of years in many cultures as a form of art, currency and decoration. Beads in all their forms, wooden, glass or clay, are always a delightful detail. I like to dress a room with jewellery – as much as I do myself – as we have with a colourful beaded lampshade in this drawing room (above).

Here are four ways we use beads to create playful and fun interiors:

**1. Change the scale**
It's always important to think big. Even when using something small and dainty like a bead, it should still create an impact, as it does on the lampshade in this London drawing room (above).

These giant mud-bead vases (right) were handmade by a collective in South Africa. We added lighting within the pots to shine through the gaps between the chalky white beads. The raw simplicity of these vases looks bold and impressive when placed in groups.

## 2. Dressing the room

Getting dressed up is always fun and it's the same for our interiors.

If I have a beautiful necklace from my travels or a string of beads that just seem to fit with the rest of the room, I often drape them over a piece of sculptural art or hang them from an unsuspecting lamp base or over a mirror (opposite, top left and right).

Using beads in this way adds another texture to the space and makes things feel more personal.

## 3. Let there be light

A lovely way to accessorise with beadwork is through lighting. I used this miniature beaded chandelier over a small breakfast table in a Suite at Crosby Street Hotel (opposite, bottom). The combination of fabric and glass beads creates an elegant pattern of light over the table below.

In the Spring Room (below left and right) hangs a chandelier of hand-pressed clay beads in a kaleidoscope of technicolour. Each mud-bead tile in the chandelier is hand-painted and stamped with a charming little design of flowers or birds. There was great excitement when it arrived, but it was a laborious process to put it safely into place.

My favourite beaded lights are these Kirdi pendant lights (left, opposite and on page 55). Made from vibrantly colourful beaded aprons, I like to hang these in clusters to make the most of the fabulous beadwork, bright colours and abundant texture they provide.

Hung in a collection at various heights in front of a window, beaded lights can also look very inviting.

### 4. Trims and embellishments

I use beaded trims on curtains and cushions (below) to add a fun accent to a room. It is something you might have to look at for a second time to even notice.

I like to think of these details as part of a room's story, like a favourite old book with little gems of prose that you might not catch the first time in reading. A room should always have a surprise on entering, and beaded trims and finishes never fail to disappoint.

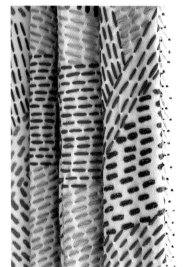

# IN THE ROUND

In the Design Studio, we are always coming up with innovative design solutions that are both practical and beautiful. Getting the balance right is key. When designing a room, the first and most important thing to consider is how guests will move through a space.

In busier public areas, I often choose round forms, allowing for multiple vantage points and an easy flow within the space. In the lobby at The Soho Hotel (opposite, top left), we decided to turn an oval painting by Joe Fan on its side to create a table. It has a clear top to protect the work, and we made a bright red Perspex base for the table legs. An array of vases of different shapes and sizes sit upon it, adding height and scale to the room.

The centrepiece is crucial for the circulation of this large transitional space, and the unexpected nature of this artwork-come-table makes it hard to forget. We have used another Joe Fan artwork to the same effect at Ham Yard Hotel (top right and bottom right).

As you move from the Drawing Room to The Orangery at The Whitby Hotel, you pass a stunning whalebone-leg table with an assortment of Katherine Cuthbert vases placed on top (opposite).

The swirling organic forms of the 'Isatis' Casamance fabric on the walls proves the perfect juxtaposition to the Crittall steel doors and the fresh flowers in the beautifully painted vases. My embroidered 'Friendly Flowers' fabric used on the curtains behind adds a bolt of colour, creating a relaxed and welcoming space.

In the lobby of the more traditional Covent Garden Hotel (above), a cane-backed *conversationé* chair leads the eye towards a dramatic dividing curtain made from antique needlepoint rugs. This combination creates a charming and theatrical entrance to the reception area, giving our guests somewhere to sit without having to overcrowd this busy space with multiple chairs.

When building Ham Yard Hotel, we commissioned the sculptor Tony Cragg to create a focal point for the outside courtyard (opposite). There is little contemporary public sculpture in London, so I felt

Cragg's fluid designs would be the perfect fit for the space. The work is called 'Group' and it required a great deal of engineering skill to piece this 4 m (12 ft) tall sculpture together.

The beauty of this work is its scale and the irregular organic forms of which it is made. It can be viewed 'in the round', making it the perfect sculpture for this transitional public space. I love to see passers-by walk around it and marvel.

# A PLACE TO PUT PEN TO PAPER

Creating cosy bedrooms, dazzling event spaces and lively restaurants is a weekly occurrence in our design studio, but an often-overlooked space is the 'study'. Our guests visit us for work and for pleasure, so we need to be imaginative with nooks and corners to create spaces where they can get down to business. I like them to have a beautiful space in which to write a theatre script, pen a novel or simply write a to-do list.

In the Penthouse Suite at Charlotte Street Hotel (opposite, top) there is a beautiful, 19th-century, French antique desk made with a variety of exotic woods – kingwood and satinwood – with gilt detailing.

Antiques add a sense of character and tell a story. It is such a luxury to sit at a beautifully crafted piece of furniture – you can imagine all the letters written at that desk.

Here, a desk next to the bed (left) has a dual function as a bedside table (nightstand). The buttery yellow desk harmonises with Judy Buxton's painting above. This old desk sits higher than usual, so I teamed it with a stool rather than a chair. The hot-pink phone adds a fabulous pop of colour.

In the Oak Leaf Suite at Ham Yard Hotel, we used a fun 'Reserve Seat Cushion' trim on the desk chair to add a playful detail to the room (left).

In an apartment at Denman Place, my 'Ozone' fabric for Christopher Farr Cloth creates a colourful backdrop to this book-lined nook (bottom left).

In another corner nook of a bedroom, the desk is tiny but lends great character, positioned below two framed contemporary illustrations and then dressed with a quirky table lamp, the base of which is made from ribbon reels (bottom right).

In a world where information is exchanged so readily, there is something nostalgic and romantic about a writing desk. In all our favourite rooms, there is always a desk to sit at, whether to work, read or simply ponder. I love the idea that these might provide unique, joyful, inspiring spaces to enjoy and entertain creative thoughts.

In the Drawing Room at Covent Garden Hotel, the detail on this antique writing desk is exquisite (above and see page 64). Very often, a room requires a hefty piece of furniture to pull it all together – this massive, old, marquetry roll-top desk, made in Japan for the European market in the 19th century, is the *pièce de résistance* in this large panelled drawing room. We contrasted this desk with a very contemporary, streamlined John Stefanidis chair, an 18th-century Swedish clock and a mid-20th-century telephone. Surprisingly, it all looks as if it has been there forever.

# CELEBRATING RAW MATERIALS

Often, when designing an interior, the hardest thing to do is nothing. Celebrating raw materials is a wonderful way of exercising restraint – the most beautiful patinas and intricate patterns can come from the natural world, but resisting the urge to add intricate detailing, which would prove counterintuitive, is a difficult task. It is important to always remember that sometimes less is more.

This petrified tree (above) stopped traffic in Manhattan when it was installed in the courtyard at Crosby Street Hotel in Soho.

On the Roof Terrace at Ham Yard Hotel, the simplicity of these wicker pendant lights, set against the urban backdrop of Central London, creates a moment of calm. Their wonderful natural imperfections are emphasised by the straight-edged brick and concrete of the metropolis beyond.

At Dorset Square Hotel, in London, the timber and stone tables designed by Tom Stogdon in the Drawing Room – where the natural, unrefined tabletops are elevated by simple architectural legs – contrast with their more tailored surroundings (above).

The vivacious monochromatic patterning of Arabescato marble, quarried in Tuscany, creates a clean yet organic feeling of luxury that is perfect for a master bathroom (right).

I work with textures and materials of all kinds, from aged oak surfaces to fresh and zippy Perspex, but one of my favourites is alabaster.

This mineral, a finely granular variety of gypsum, is soft and versatile, making it ideal for carving and sculpting into elaborate forms. Alabaster can be translucent or opaque, proving an excellent material for lighting because it creates a soft inviting glow. Here are a few ways we have used alabaster in our designs.

We commissioned a chandelier for the Terrace Suite at Ham Yard Hotel (above left and overleaf). The smooth, simple alabaster balls dance around one another, suspended from protruding metal rods wrapped in twine. It provides a balance of both delicacy and strength,

as well as emanating a wonderful warmth which is so important for any chandelier.

When I first found this alabaster sculpture triptych by the artist Stephen Cox (above right) at a Royal Academy Summer Exhibition, I knew instantly that it had to sit pride of place in The Whitby Hotel's lobby.

This figurative upright sculpture of three female forms is a showcase of alabaster in all its glory, smooth in places yet granulated and textured in others. It is a swirl of pattern, a surface you just want to explore. Again, it shows a balance that is at once delicate yet robust and strong. This piece was so heavy that it took eight men to move each section into position and we even had to reinforce the floor.

# THE RULES OF MAGIC

**Magic, in all its beguiling and uplifting expressions, has always been an inspiration in my designs. Sometimes, a good interior just needs a small reference to mysticism to encourage a captivated curiosity.**

Here are some of the very subtle and underlying themes I like to play with in any room:

### MOONDOG

'Moondog' is perhaps one of my all-time favourite designs. The little dog looking through the telescope at a smiling full moon is fantastically whimsical and wonderful.

The design can sit on many types of ground cloth depending upon the use, from occasional cushions to heavy duty chairs and headboards.

## FROM THE APOTHECARY

There is always something magical about an apothecary jar, filled with beautiful plants, fragrant potions and unusual, sometimes mysterious, ingredients.

I often place these artworks by Mimi de Biarritz – in the form of beautifully crafted decorative cloches filled with colourful mushrooms, starfish or flowers (above left) – in some of our grander rooms. Even in the most luxurious space, I like to introduce a little whimsy and intrigue to remind people that design doesn't always have to be serious.

In the public stairwell at Crosby Street Hotel, lined with Kate Blee's 'Tribe' wallpaper, I have hung pop artist Joe Tilson's *Demeter*, an oil and wood diptych that plays on the symbolism of the Greek goddess who watched over the harvest, the earth's fertility and the seasons (above right).

## MYTHICAL CREATURES

My 'Mythical Creatures' range was originally developed as part of a collection with Chelsea Textiles (as used on this headboard, left).

In Charlotte Street Hotel (bottom left and right), the whimsical world of my creatures comes to life in their own folkloric landscape. It is very pleasing to know they have somewhere fun to roam.

My mythical creatures, derived from mythology, folklore and ancient textiles, evoke magic, mystery and charm, and I love how they seem to spring up everywhere.

In my collection of fabrics and wallpapers with Andrew Martin, and at my pop-up on the seventh floor of the Bergdorf Goodman department store in New York (above and right), these prancing creatures were ever-present.

Across the headboard and bed cushions, appliquéd creatures such as a Flying Antelope and Mr Gherkin, the dog, leap across mythical lands, taking in trees richly laden with pears and fields filled with flowers.

Generous sofas upholstered in the patchwork pattern of dragons, unicorns and spotted leopards prancing between strawberry bushes and fruit trees of my 'Hedgerow Quince' design created a painterly, fairy-tale allure. It's always fun to bring in a humorous twist of the things you love to make your home unique to you .

We admire so many, we only have
space for so few

# MEET THE MAKER

Margit Wittig | Joe Fan

Colin Millington | OK David

Martha Freud | Katherine Cuthbert

Clio Peppiatt | Mimi De Biarritz

# MARGIT WITTIG

Margit Wittig is a German-born, London-based sculptor, painter and designer-maker of contemporary bespoke lighting, screens and occasional furniture. I love Margit's figurative lamp designs, which come in an array of materials such as bronze, clay, resin, glass and jesmonite and are inspired by studying the human form in her previous career as a physiotherapist.

When Margit first started, I snapped up her table lamps because I knew they would be perfect for the Anrep Room at The Whitby Hotel. Here she tells us about her inspirations:

*You trained and worked as a physiotherapist, what made you move into the design world?*
I have always been artistic. I grew up in a very creative environment – my mother was an artist and I remember painting watercolours of our garden with her, or every year before Christmas we collected old candles to melt the wax to cast festive ornaments, filling the house with a wonderful aroma.

I trained as a physiotherapist but stopped working when we moved to the US in 1997. When I returned to London a few years later, as a young mother of two, I wanted a more creative outlet, so first I studied figurative sculpting and then metalwork at art school. I fell totally in love with it and over the years I have developed my own abstract style.

In the beginning, I transformed my sculpted heads, along with other shapes in resin and handblown glass, into lamps simply as a hobby. I made myself a floor lamp and then one for a table; then my first orders were from friends, but soon my designs were noticed by interior designers too.

*How would you describe your work?*
Kit once described my designs as 'curious, intriguing, classical, yet lyrical'. I would say my work is sculptural and functional. I enjoy designing new pieces that have a purpose, like lighting, tables, tabletops, door handles and room dividers, but enriching them with artistic components to transform each one into a unique object.

*Where do you find inspiration for the craftsmanship of your lamps?*
Inspiration comes from many sources; for example, the forms of my figurines are informed by the sculptures of Brâncuși and Giacometti. Funnily enough, everyone says that I turned lighting into art, in fact. I am very fond of texture. On dog walks or gallery visits, I take

snapshots of the barks of trees or zoom into paintings to look closely at the brushstrokes. This inspires my own work as I like to create a unique organic texture by applying different layers of patina to add depth.

*In recent years, you have expanded your collection into making and designing tables, mirrors, screens and even door handles. What is your favourite piece to make and why?*
I'll always be busy making new lampstands and I love to work on different designs, but I recently designed a cube-shaped occasional table, which can also be used as a stool. The original was made of clay with imprints of tree bark – I'm looking forward to casting it in bespoke colours.

*You use many different materials in your work. What do you most like to work with and why?*
Although I use a lot of materials in my work, clay is always my first choice because it is wonderfully versatile. I can really mess around with it to create shape and texture, but if the thing I'm making gets a bit exhausted or doesn't work out, I can simply squash it together and start again. I don't like to waste materials. I use clay to make the moulds for my resin sculptures as well as for developing ideas.

*Do you have a favourite piece of work you have created over the years?*
A favourite piece is a screen I designed because it was one of my first large-scale creations. It displays many different sculptural

components and can be used as a room divider or just as a decorative piece of functional art. The interchangeable resin elements – shaped like large pearls, sculptural birds in flight and silhouettes of heads – can be rotated to give it a new and changing appearance, creating a different 'look' every time. As with my other pieces, a variety of components can be chosen in different colours and positioned to create a completely bespoke screen.

# JOE FAN

'The Wine Drinker', in all his glory, hangs in this busy New York brasserie

**We are huge fans of Joe Fan for the quality, subtlety and detail of his work. As a figurative painter, Joe paints contemplative, intriguing, imagined landscapes, woven with humorous, joyful narratives, which draw on the influences of Medieval tapestries, ancient Chinese painting and Renaissance art.**

In London's Ham Yard Bar & Restaurant, I have hung Joe's outstanding artworks *The Painter* (2014) and the diptych *Family Outing* (2014). The soft undertones of these paintings work well with the strong yellow and orange hues decorating the space, adding a calm touch of surrealism to this dynamic scheme.

In New York, the enormous height of the Crosby Bar's ceilings meant we could overscale the pictures. We installed two of Joe's very large oil paintings, including a dream-like feast to whet the appetite. *The Wine Drinker* (opposite, top) was the perfect fit for the restaurant.

An unexpected way of contemplating Joe's work has involved transforming his paintings into modern tabletops, such as in the lift area at The Soho Hotel (above). At Ham Yard Hotel, *A Winter's Tale*, depicting people climbing ladders and trees into other worlds, works wonderfully as a tabletop in the entrance (see page 61). For both, bold Perspex legs were designed as a base to make each piece really stand out.

Joe was born in Hong Kong in 1962 but moved to Scotland in the late 1970s, later applying for a place at Gray's School of Art at Robert Gordon University to study Fine Art. After much acclaim and numerous prizes, Joe continues to live and work in Aberdeen. He is also a member of the Scottish Royal Academy.

Here, Joe talks about his work and inspiration:

*The art world is a complicated one, when did you start to paint?*
I was always drawing when I was young – my mum told me she often found my doodling all over the family furniture! It was when I came to Aberdeen, first to study English as a foreign student, then graphic design, that I discovered Gray's School of Art. At that point, I decided that drawing and painting was what I wanted to do, so, in 1984, I began a four-year Honours degree course.

*Where do you find inspiration?*
I've always been interested in the early Renaissance artists, whose landscapes often looked carefully designed, constructed and 'staged'. In my work, the recurring use of the 'garden' theme is very much inspired and influenced by that particular manner of thinking.

*When we admire your paintings, they feel dream-like and melancholic. What do you aim to express?*
I work mostly from my imagination and my landscapes are not based on any particular place. Perhaps that is why my paintings have this other-worldly, dream-like, surreal ambience about them.

Painting is a solitary pursuit and I often spend days on my own in the studio. My work is sometimes about the narrative of one's journey through life. This reflects a melancholy mood which appears naturally in my work.

The different aspects of genre painting, such as landscape, still life and portraiture, have always been of interest to me.

I particularly admire artists who have their own personal take on their subject – for example, Cézanne's apples, Van Gogh's chair and Picasso's portrait. In my work, I am trying to do the same and to create something of my own.

*You were a lecturer before dedicating yourself full-time to painting. Do you have any advice on making the jump?*
I was offered a teaching job two years after I graduated from Gray's and I taught there for about 10 years. I enjoyed working with the students and find that my own work greatly benefitted from that experience.

# COLIN MILLINGTON

Colin Millington's work captures everything I love about handcrafted pieces. Each artwork is unique and filled with so much intrigue and detail. These lyrical and whimsical woolwork illustrations (above), which feature in many of my room designs, feel intricate and historical, and yet they are wonderfully modern.

Colin has based his work on the nautical tradition of British sailors practising crafts while away at sea. A retired sailor, now living on the Norfolk coast, Colin's embroidered characters dance across sandy beaches and boats sail across whale-filled seas.

Here Colin reflects on the inspirations behind his complex woolworks:

*Your needlepoint depicts both English settings and far-off lands. Are you inspired by your own travels or is it all from your imagination?*
**It comes from both really. I spent most of my life in the Royal Navy and Merchant Navy, travelling the world from North and South America to India, Japan and Australia, down the east and west coasts of Africa and through both the Panama and Suez canals.**

**During my later years as a Coast Guard, I watched how the sea met the shore and this now often features in my work. I also look at historical sources, old prints and Victorian pottery, and of course old sailors' woolworks for ideas.**

*In these modern times, with machinery often overtaking skilled crafts, how do you see this style continuing and how can we keep it alive?*
**Machines will never replace handwork as they are too precise and lack the ability to improvise. Sometimes I will run out of a colour of wool that I might be using for the sea, so I pick another colour which changes the overall effect. I often start with a drawing, but as I work, the idea develops and grows.**

**To keep it alive, we need to get back to teaching handwork at school and at home. The girls in my family were always taught to knit by their mothers. Children need to see us working, so they become interested.**

Colin's pieces are reminiscent of the work of Cornish artist (and fisherman) Alfred Wallis as well as the 19th-century tradition of 'Woolies', for which sailors used scraps of coloured wool to embroider pictures of sailing ships. In the Suffolk Suite at Haymarket Hotel (above), I bordered one of Colin's artworks with a simple white frame to contrast with the lively mix of colour and texture in the embroidery, and to help introduce a 'stitched' theme to the design scheme.

*How did you discover the craft?*
Seamen could always use a needle. When I was first at sea as an apprentice on a tramp steamer, we had to hand-sew the canvas hatch covers to keep out the weather. Many years later, I saw an old woolwork in an antique shop window and simply thought I would have a go at copying one. It just developed from there.

*Each work tells a completely different story. How do you start telling those stories? Is it inspiration from an object or a tale you have been told?*
Of course, I have been told hundreds of tales during my time at sea, and now I read books, but often it is looking at pictures of old ships that is

the starting point. My motifs are always nautical, with coastlines, compasses and flags – and at least one ship in every picture.

*The works are made up of so many textures – is there a special wool and technique that you use to create this?*
I use Appletons two-ply pure yarn. They are an old English company and make over four hundred different colours. I mostly work using simple long and short stitch, but sometimes chain stitch, and I might add in details with silk and occasionally glass beads. My style is naïve, traditional, quite rough and ready.

*How long do your works usually take?*
I mostly work in the evenings, for perhaps two or three hours, and a picture will take between one and two weeks.

*When was your big break?*
I used to sell a few from the boot of my car until one day, a few years ago, I offered one to Luke

Scott of the gallery Paffron & Scott – who I knew from the days of running a junk shop with my wife – and he liked them so much that he has promoted and sold my pictures ever since.

*Where can we see your work?*
Apart from Kit's hotels, the Sheringham Museum, in Norfolk.

# OK DAVID

OK David is an illustrator, painter, designer and writer. I just love his whimsical characters and witty sense of humour. He is the brainchild behind the best-selling fabric design for Liberty's 'Queue for the Zoo'. We have a collection of David's *12 Dancers* paintings in the Dive Bar at Ham Yard Hotel (above), which are sure to inspire some pretty epic dance moves.

*Like me, you clearly enjoy working with vibrant colours – what are your favourite colour combinations and why?*

Yes, I can't help loving colour. I love how simple it is on the surface, and how rich it is when you go deeper and see how it's not one single colour at all.

I have a special love for greens and certain intense blues, but I don't have a favourite combination. Putting colours in different settings completely alters their effect.

It's surprising how much impact a colour can have,

and how it can change your mood.

I tend to think of colours as characters in a story. The special chemistry of colours lies in their tones.

*You have such a wild imagination, where do you find your inspiration?*
**Sometimes something speaks to me, and then I keep asking myself why I like it until I have my answer. I am a story person. I am always looking for an escape route into a story or onto an interesting train of thought. When I look at something, I see the colours and the composition of the shapes, but what I am trying to find is a narrative, and if it's a funny story, that's even better.**

*You have recently become a full-time artist/designer, starting your business OK David. Do you have any advice on making the jump?*
**For me, it's more of a hop, skip and then a jump. I'm at the skip part at the moment. I'm doing lots of commissions and designs for other people, but I haven't launched my own designs yet.**

*It's such a fine line when creating characters and designs which are whimsical and folky, yet not too child-like or cartoony – how do you know when you have got a design just right?*

Everyone has their own tastes, so that fine line is a very wiggly wriggly one. For me, something is more or less right when it doesn't feel wrong. Perhaps it's like adding salt when you're cooking. You have to keep tasting it.

I want to evoke a feeling of something. If I look at what I've made and I feel some spark of feeling, then I know I'm getting close.

*When starting a commission, what are your usual steps?*
**People commission me to design fabric patterns, and to make paintings. As well as**

Bill

understanding the commission – what's it for, where's it for, when's it for? – I like to understand the person who is commissioning me. What do they like? What brings them joy, and what makes them laugh?

When I work with Liberty, I have a lot of freedom, which is how I like it. They tell me what the theme of the collection is, and they let me find my own take. When I did 'Queue for the Zoo' (above left), they just asked for animals. I added all the clothes and hats because I thought that would be more interesting.

For 'Dapper Dogs', which showed lots of dogs at a party (including Bill, a Portuguese street dog sporting a chicken walking stick and a bone-patterned waistcoat, above right), the only change was to do with the dogs drinking wine and smoking cigars. Apparently, that's no good for a children's fabric!

When I painted *12 Dancers* for Ham Yard Hotel (opposite and previous page), I wrote the names of the dancers and what they were dancing to on the back of each painting. While I was painting them, I was listening to a lot of Fats Waller

and other music from that time. There is always a secret story that connects me to what I've made.

# MARTHA FREUD

Martha Freud is a London-based ceramicist whose delicate glowing pots and pendant lights can be spotted in many of the spaces we have designed in London and New York.

At Ham Yard Hotel, the restaurant could have been a long and dark space, but we added dimension and light on the back wall with a delicate collection of pots.

Martha's glowing handmade ceramic pots, set into 32 niches against a crisp white backdrop, create a calm wall in a busy room. Each one is inscribed with an individual leaf design and lit up to give a warm glow as you dine below.

In The Potting Shed restaurant at Dorset Square Hotel (see page 99, bottom), we have hung Martha's beautifully crafted butterfly lights in each of the banquette seating alcoves and in front of the zinc-topped bar. In homage to the history of Dorset Square, which was once the site of Thomas Lord's first cricket ground, we also have 192 handmade ceramic pots by Martha, which light up with cricketing sayings such as 'How to cure a cricketer's red nose – drink 'til it's purple', and of course, Richard Bernard's famous quote, 'That's a contradiction in terms'.

Here Martha answers a few questions about her work:

*Where is your favourite place to find inspiration?*
**I'm a sponge to my environment, so I take inspiration from wherever I am. I love to be in nature, ideally on a long walk in the woods or on a beach. It is so meditative for me to walk with no purpose – that is when I am most open to being inspired.**

**When I am in the city for long stretches, the way humans interact with each other ends up being more of a focus and becomes where my ideas play. I try to notice when something makes me laugh or positively motivates me, as these are the things I want to encourage.**

*In The Whitby Hotel's Orangery, 40 illuminated porcelain pots are etched with landmark buildings and bridges in New York (below). Your pieces are all so different yet share a common thread. How do you take unique ideas and translate them into each piece?*
**As an artist I try to interpret the essence of my inspiration rather than attempt a realistic representation – I love working with ceramics because they are so adaptable, but I like to let the idea dictate the material, rather than the other way round. I enjoy taking an idea from one place and trying it somewhere else to see how it looks from a different perspective.**

In the Reading Room at The Whitby Hotel, your tulip ceramic pendant lights line the ceiling, creating a focal point in the room (above). Your work consists of beautiful textures and weights, why are you so drawn to clay?

It can be such a beautifully natural and earthy process working with clay. To then contrast the delicate rawness of ceramics with the weight of manufactured steel, and to find complementary harmony between these two materials, is a

theme I keep coming back to – perhaps because it mirrors the challenging balance many of us urban dwellers are trying to find in ourselves today.

*How do you know when a piece is finished?*
I love to re-work pieces and constantly try to grow and challenge myself, each time pushing the materials or technique further to see what can be done; but sometimes it is knowing that the right thing is to stop or strip it back to allow space for personal interpretation. Some projects have taken me years as I develop the right skills to manifest my ideas, while others have happened really quickly.

# KATHERINE CUTHBERT

**Katherine Cuthbert is a multidisciplinary London-based artist whose work I have avidly collected for many years. Her combinations of tall, smooth and graphic pots mixed in with organic, stalagmite-like vases are very sculptural and always look so striking teamed together in a curated collection.**

I love to use her work in entranceways, welcoming people into the space and evoking a sense of home, but also providing a point of interest to catch the eye. To me, her work has delicacy yet always a punchy graphic twist. Whether it's a bold shock of gold around a delicately painted flower or a 'cut here' scissors symbol up a pot or around a bowl, she brings in the unexpected in a really clever way.

is one of my favourite flowers. I go into my studio at about 7 a.m. and start preparing a board for fresco painting. I grind all my own natural pigments – their colours are so vibrant and beautiful, a real pleasure to work with. While I wait for the lime plaster to dry to the required dampness, I start making pots. I love working with clay, a material created from the breakdown of granite over millions of years, so soft and malleable, then transformed back into a rock-like hardness by the volcanic temperature of the kiln.

*Tell us about your creative process?*
My work is all done by throwing on a slow turning wheel, with very soft clay, which allows my hands and the wheel to become one, working together in harmony.

I first started painting with acrylics, but it wasn't very satisfactory, so I learned how to do proper fresco, painting with pigments onto wet lime plaster which become chemically bound so it looks like coloured stone. It is a wonderful technique to work with.

Here Katherine delves into her world to discuss her process and the creative tools she can't live without:

*What does a day in the life of Katherine Cuthbert look like?*
I am an early riser – I get up at 5 a.m. because I love the stillness of that time in the morning, and I often start the day by going for a walk in the local park, taking my sketchbook. I found a pomegranate bush there a few weeks ago and the vermillion flowers, with their thin, crumpled petals glowing in the dawn sunrise, were a lovely surprise, as it

I like to paint onto leather-hard pots and then fire them before the glaze, but sometimes I paint with oxides on a biscuit pot because it will run more and that's the effect I want. As my pots are about providing a container for flowers, I use only black and white because colour would take away from the vibrancy of the flowers.

For me, making pots and painting are intertwined. Each brings different and exciting challenges, and I really enjoy the physicality of working with different materials.

*When did your career as an artist begin?*
I have always loved making things. As child I made collages because the materials were easy to get hold of – just old magazines and glue. When I was 19, I started working with needlepoint, first making handbags and then pictures. I took some to the Portal Gallery, in London, and was represented by them for many years after that. I never think of what I do as a career, as making is just something I love doing. It is simply the way I live.

*Where do you find inspiration?*
Mainly in nature – this wonderful earth provides so much inspiration. I am also inspired by 14th- and 15th-century Italian artists, like Giotto, Masaccio, Taddeo Gaddi and especially Simone Martini, whose techniques in fresco painting show his constant explorations and experiments.

*What do you hope people get from seeing you work?*
I think that in my work, I look for that quiet moment of stillness and simplicity, but I also like to explore the

quirkiness of contradictions and impossibilities, such as in my 'cut here' pots. When I am making, I am completely absorbed in the process, where that tranquil time becomes my world – I hope that moment of calm absorption, that serenity, might resonate with people who see my work.

*Your ceramics are some of our most coveted pieces in the rooms. When did you start making them and what sparked the inspiration?*
I started making pots in my early 30s. I saw some of Lucie Rie's pots and was struck by their beauty and simplicity. I was so inspired that I immediately joined a pottery evening class. After a couple of weeks there, I wrote to her and she invited me to her mews house where I spent a magical day with her. After that, I went to see her once a week to show her the pots I had made. It was a very precious time.

*Where is your studio? What kind of space is it?*
My studio is in my home. Years ago, I rented a studio space, but I couldn't work in it. I arrived in the morning and felt constrained, boxed in somehow, so after a

year I gave it up and set up a studio at home. It is a big room, overlooking gardens filled with birds, squirrels and foxes. A wonderful room to work in, as it feels rather like a treehouse.

*If you were on a desert island what one thing would you choose as your luxury item?*
An endless supply of sketchbooks, pencils and drawing pens.

*What advice would you give to any budding creatives out there?*
Be adventurous, experiment and explore, and look at everything you can. Inspiration is everywhere. Listen to what people say about your work, but mainly trust in yourself because you are unique.

# CLIO PEPPIATT

**Clio Peppiatt is a sustainable fashion designer, based in London, who creates highly individual clothes that last.**

With her handcrafted and forward-thinking approach, I thought she would be perfect to collaborate with for making a headboard, bed cushions and sofa cushions for the Terrace Suite at The Soho Hotel, inspired by the rich, vibrant history of the local Soho music scene.

I worked closely with Clio on the project, culminating in the creation of an impressive 3 x 3-m (10 x 10-ft), hand-embroidered headboard and accompanying soft furnishings.

I admire Clio's completely unique style – her skilful and intricate beadwork, combined with electric, rough silks and frills, tell us a story and bring the fun back to fashion.

Without relying on traditional feminine and masculine stereotypes, Clio creates clothes that focus on female empowerment. Before starting her own business, she worked with the British fashion house Alexander McQueen.

When I met at her design studio, Clio was wearing a vintage Vivienne Westwood corset under a wonderful, own-brand, snakeskin-effect PVC, ankle-length jacket with a violet-blue faux fur collar and cuffs. Obviously, it was love at first sight!

*What sparks your imagination and inspires a collection?*

**Originally, I come from a fine art background, which still has a strong influence on what inspires my designs. Recently, I've been looking at Victorian fairy paintings. They are just so enchanting and remind me of a William Blake exhibition I saw recently, which I loved. My imagination is always sparked by that type of esoteric, magical storytelling.**

**I'm a lover of traditional craftsmanship, which is the other predominant influence on my work. I was born in Paris and grew up in a home surrounded by art and artists. My great-grandmother was a lacemaker, specialising in women's gloves, and I was taught to embroider by my Grandma, so craft has always been very close to my heart. Preserving those skills is really important to me, but I try to do it in an original way that makes sense in our modern world, usually with a sense of playfulness and touch of the surreal.**

*Do you have a colour palette you always go back to or is it constantly evolving and changing?*
In the past, I've often returned to pinks, reds and lilacs as I see them as colours associated with a traditional femininity which can then be contrasted with a tailored silhouette or a motif that subverts that idea. I often work with raw silk taffetas, made from the leftover pulp from spinning fine silks. They have a gorgeous luminosity that works well with rich, indulgent colours.

*You are an advocate for sustainability in fashion. Is it challenging to find brightly coloured textiles which are ethically made, sustainable and durable?*
It's very difficult! Last year I started to work with an expert sustainable weaver and dyer in India and I couldn't believe the range of possibilities

compared to when I started five years ago. I feel hopeful that as the world becomes more aware of this issue, there will be even more developments on this front.

*The headboard you've made for the master bedroom in the Terrace Suite at The Soho Hotel (opposite) is like an artwork in itself, so lyrical and beautifully made. What inspired its motifs?*
Soho's illustrious musical past, as a vibrant hub for London's music halls and nightclubs as well as being home to recording studios which have been graced by the likes of the Rolling Stones and David Bowie, inspired the idea of musical instruments, especially as they worked so well with traditional, almost folkloric-looking, embroidery techniques.

Complete with hand-dyed, golden, silk ribbon strings for the musical instruments, a three-dimensional curling feather for the bow and arrow, music scrolls inspired by Debussy's Clair de Lune, and a delicately star-stitched moon, each motif shaped in felted British wool was hand-embroidered in my London studio, using many of the stitches my Grandma taught me as a child.

Creating something for an interior was both fun and a challenge. There are so many things to take into account when designing something that someone will sleep under, like not using sequins and beading, which I do in my fashion designs, because I didn't want people to get their hair caught. So, an embroidered theme of old-fashioned instruments, including a mandolin, trumpet and Grecian lyre, as well Cupid bows, the sun, moon and stars, felt calming and harmonious.

# MIMI DE BIARRITZ

Mimi de Biarritz is a French artist living and working in Biarritz. Mimi shares an Atelier with Pioche Projects and always seems to have her finger on the pulse with humorous, intricate pieces using cardboard cut-outs, mixed media printing, papier-mâché, needlepoint, mosaics and furniture design.

If it inspires Mimi, she will give it a go. She is fearless and a true craftswoman. Once a year I go specially to Biarritz to visit Mimi and to see what wonderful creations she has been working on.

Handmade miniature theatres, stitched jackets and appliqué flags are crammed into every corner. Wonderful painted furniture pieces have papier-mâché vivariums placed on top, with cardboard cut-out chandeliers dangling above and curious collections sitting below. Her work provides a treasure trove we feel incredibly lucky to have discovered. There is no one in the world quite like Mimi de Biarritz!

*You use so many different mediums, what is your favourite and why?*
**I feel lucky to love working with all kinds of different materials. I can't say which one I prefer. When I'm tired of embroidery, I switch to painting or paper cut-outs or shells. I never ever get bored or lack ideas.**

*Did you study art?*
**No, although when I was 18 years old, following classical studies, I wanted to go to the Beaux Arts School, but my**

mother told me I would probably die of hunger like most artists, so I followed her wise advice.

*Are you inspired by other artists?*
Of course! So many artists, past and present, inspire me, including Matisse, Dalí and Picasso, but also Basquiat, Banksy and many more. They give me constant creative nourishment.

*In your opinion, what is the difference between art and craft?*
In my mind, there is no difference. The cave wall paintings of the Neanderthals are masterpieces, just as stunning and moving as a delicate 18th-century oil painting. Craft can be art just as some art can be ... terrible!

*What is the typical day in the life of Mimi?*
Coffee, cigarettes, music and lots of projects to be finalised ...

*I know you love flea markets and treasure hunting – what has been your best find?*
It's difficult to say. Each time I find something that fits a nebulous project in the back of my mind, I'm thrilled, but I have a soft spot for the dusty maquette of the Titanic that I found at a flea market. It was obviously waiting for me to rescue it and give it a proper stage.

*Do you like travelling and does this inspire your artwork?*
I have travelled a lot. Now I travel on the internet and discover wonderful crafts and places that are so inspiring. I have never been to Russia, but I saw the beautiful, lace-like, painted wooden houses that inspired me to create the coloured bird boxes (below).

*Who is your hero?*
I don't have a hero but I'm sure the world is full of heroes, although totally anonymous!

*Always say 'Yes' whenever possible, rather than 'No' — go for it!*

# DO'S AND DON'TS

# THE POWER OF PAINT

I am known for lining walls with padded fabric or beautifully patterned wallpaper. However, I never overlook the power of flat emulsion paint. Today, we are spoilt for choice – you can visit any local DIY store and browse through countless shades and hues of every colour in the rainbow. Here are my suggested do's and don'ts for paint:

**1. DO consider the space**
First consider the area you are painting and how you want to feel in that space. You might want a restful colour scheme in the bedroom and something punchier in the living room.

Ambient light changes throughout the day and causes colours to transform. In east-

and west-facing rooms, the light changes more dramatically, so make sure you know how a colour looks and feels in both the morning and afternoon.

### 2. DON'T forget to sample

Your favourite colour might not be the best for the room you are painting due to its aspect. Sometimes painting directly onto the wall doesn't work because the sample paint reacts with the existing wall colour. Instead, paint your sample onto a large piece of card or wood which you can move around the room at different times of the day.

### 3. DON'T be afraid to be bold

A strong background colour creates contrast and makes a space interesting. In Ham Yard Hotel's Drawing Room (overleaf, top), I have used a dark umber hue on the walls. Here, I used a fabric to line the walls, but if budget is an issue, a strong paint colour can create the same impact. When the colour is going up, keep your nerve. Remember that when you add curtains, artworks, fabric and people to the room, the walls will no longer be the only focus.

### 4. DON'T think white is boring

On the other hand, don't dismiss white – it can be a very powerful colour, especially when teamed with a vibrant abstract painting and the grainy texture of a sculptural oak bench and wide-planked floors (above). In the Ham Yard Bar & Restaurant, I painted the back wall white to allow the 32 glowing porcelain pots by Martha Freud (see page 96), each tucked into its own niche, to take centre stage.

### 5. DO consider the environment and your health

Traditional painting methods and materials can be harmful to the environment. Look for paints with a low VOC (Volatile Organic Compound) rating – these significantly reduce the

*We loved this so much, we made it in miniature!*

amount of toxic vapour being released into your home, ensuring better air quality and no strong odours.

Paint brands that are kinder to the planet include Little Greene, which manufactures water- and vegetable oil-based paints; Earthborn's Claypaints and Eggshell Emulsions are free from acrylics, oils and smells; and Edward Bulmer offers a paint range that uses natural pigments, in a gorgeous array of colours, which are worth the slightly heftier price tag.

### 6. DO mix and match

If you have a dado rail, consider combining wallpaper and paint – it allows you to invest

in a wonderful wallpaper for above the dado rail while using a lighter neutral paint below. This keeps the room from feeling too busy as well as helping to keep down the cost.

### 7. DO try specialist techniques

At Charlotte Street Hotel, the panelled walls in the library are painted with a 'Strié' technique (opposite, bottom). This technique mimics the look of centuries-old paint where the bristle marks are visible. It gives the room a sense of history. You would never know that the panelling is MDF (Medium Density Fibreboard) and not the real thing.

### 8. DON'T forget fun accents

Add a splash of colour. I love to create surprise by painting a shocking yellow or red inside a wardrobe or dressing room, or even a bright turquoise across the ceiling, as I did for a house with a tropical vibe (see page 114).

### 9. DO paint a mural

At Charlotte Street Hotel, I commissioned the artist Alexander Hollweg to paint a mural in the Oscar Bar & Restaurant (above), depicting contemporary London life in the year 2000 when the hotel opened, but in the style of British artist Duncan Grant's murals, which also depict daily life, but in the early 20th century.

Paint is easy to use, easy to change and there is so much choice out there, so pick up a paintbrush and get creative!

# BEHIND THE CURTAIN

Over the centuries, there have been many different styles for dressing windows. From ornate swags and tails to wave-headed minimalism. I usually prefer a full-length curtain with a single goblet pleat heading. This type of heading gives a classic finish that is neither contemporary nor traditional, with a regular fold which isn't too structured or fussy.

There are plenty of ways to come up with new and exciting curtain designs. Here is my list of do's and don'ts when you're designing your own:

### 1. DO go for a large-scale print

Curtains are the perfect place to use a 'wow factor' large-scale print that you love. Bold prints are best used on tall curtains, so you can see a good amount of the repeat. I love a wide geometric design. In the Terrace Suite at The Soho Hotel (above), I used Hazelton House's 'Chainstitch' fabric on the curtains. This is an old block print design from their archives, which I had recoloured, and it's amazing how much the design changed when used as a lighter linen version for the curtains. It drapes like a dream and I couldn't resist running a Kate Spade trim on the leading edge for a playful pop of contrast.

### 2. DO get creative

I always encourage creativity with curtains. In the Drawing Room at Covent Garden Hotel (opposite), I have used flags along the top of the curtains which creates a point of interest and brings sunshine-yellow light flooding into the room. There are so many options out there, so don't be afraid to have some fun. Curtains are a great opportunity to add colour and pattern to any scheme.

### 3. DON'T be afraid of a pelmet

A pelmet is a stiffened and shaped fabric that covers the top of the curtains. Pelmets are often thought to be old-fashioned and fussy; however, in the right setting and with the right fabrics they can finish off a pair of curtains perfectly.

In the library at Knightsbridge Hotel (opposite, bottom), Peter Dunham's big and beautiful paisley 'Samarkand' looks great against the strong warm linen walls. The pelmet offers a chance to admire the pattern repeat without the curtain folds and also helps to frame the bay window.

## 4. DON'T forget the detail

My love of detail applies equally to curtains, especially when added to the leading edge, whether it be a braid, trim, piping or contrast fabric.

In a suite at Crosby Street Hotel in New York (see page 122), I used a jangly, bronze beaded trim against the fresh green and

white of Blithfield's 'Oakleaves' fabric to create a cleaner look.

## 5. DO use solid colours

In the Oak Leaf suite at Ham Yard Hotel (above), I had great fun using Etamine's 'Voyage a Tunis' wallpaper which features camels and sand dunes. This adventurous walling works well with the plain burnt orange curtain finished with a lovely blue and beaded trim.

At Number Sixteen (right), the dramatic red curtains make a bold statement.

I wouldn't typically use a deep red for curtains but in this room, the full-length windows and wonderful natural light allow the dark and punchy colour to make a real statement.

# Simple but thought through

At Crosby Street Hotel (above), white linen was used for the curtains but given a punch of colour with a fun, green and navy, zigzag collage edge. This makes the curtains an interesting design feature, whether open or closed.

# DESIGN DETAIL: LEADING EDGES

**Whether in a bedroom, a living room or even a bathroom, a beautiful set of curtains can bring just as much to a scheme as the furniture.**

When it comes to curtains, a 'leading edge' is the border of the curtain which meets in the middle of the window. It can become a feature in

its own right – it's these tiny details that can capture the imagination and make a room interesting

A contrasting panel of fabric along the leading edge brings a playful pop of colour to an otherwise simple curtain. Here, a cream full-length curtain is trimmed with a pop of Seema Krish's 'Breach Candy' fabric (above); while in another room (left), a block of fiery orange, against cool formal grey linen, separated with a smart contrast of leather piping cord, creates a powerful and tailored feel.

In the Two Bedroom Crosby Suite (right), the leading edge is trimmed with a bronze beading which adds a handmade and tactile quality to the scheme.

## It's the devil in the detail that makes a room memorable

At The Soho Hotel (above), a geometric, indigoblue fabric used along the leading edge of a crisp white curtain draws the eye to the sunlight flooding through the impressive windows. This Jim Thompson fabric edging looks just as good on a fabric trim as it would do on a lampshade, helping to echo the smart blues and graphic patterns throughout the scheme.

In the Townhouse at Haymarket Hotel (see page 124), I wanted to create a curtain that lent warmth to the scheme, while highlighting the stunning floor-to-ceiling Regency windows which are the room's best features. As you can see here, I like to sit curtains back from the window so that every inch of natural light can filter into the room.

The curtains, in Soane's 'Paisley Parrot', were given a playful twist with 'French Jumbo Ric Rac' doubled up in constrasting colours.

# DRESSING SHELVES

In a wonderful room, you will see pockets of treasures, collected from far and wide. Whether these are jewel-coloured apothecary vases, shell-covered trinkets, old watering cans or Chinoiserie urns, they can be arranged in a thousand different ways.

Here are some top tips for styling your shelves:

### 1. DO treat the display as if you are designing a scheme

Think about colour, balance, texture and weight. Piling too much onto one shelf will allow objects to get lost. Choose a main feature, even if it's a small one, and work around it.

For example, at my pop-up at Bergdorf Goodman in New York, the shelves were painted in Farrow & Ball's 'Red Earth' to allow the contents of the tiers – the sharp, fresh greens of the books, the electric blues of the cardboard theatrical displays and the creamy hues from the linen cushions – to really shine.

In this library (below), a montage of boats, a New York policeman and wooden fish are set within one of the bookshelves. On another, a collection of whimsical glass domes encasing palm trees and princesses transports you from midtown Manhattan to other dreamy worlds.

### 2. DO think about balance

Using objects that are all the same size will look too uniform and military. Instead, opt for a varying range of heights and position these so that the space has a more natural balance.

Shelves do not need to have perfect symmetry, but make sure one side doesn't overpower the other. Put books next to sculptures, ornaments next to plant pots.

In this Chelsea project (above), we have dressed the shelves exactly how they should be – full of love. A childhood Humpty Dumpty watches over potted succulents and a plaster relief of a lion's head below; among favourite books, there are scented candles and vintage carpentry tools.

Think about the colours and material of the things you want to display – pair light-coloured glass with heavy stone pieces, or darker wooden frames with spindly metal ornaments.

On this stunning bleached oak antique dresser in The Orangery at The Whitby Hotel (opposite), I have placed old glass bottles in front of a backdrop of mirrored glass. A varying range of heights, glass colours and floral contents creates a beautifully soft and romantic feel.

If you have a collection of a certain item – get them out. Whether you have three of something, used as a table centrepiece, or a collection of 12 used as an intriguing feature along a top shelf, playing with multiples is a great way to create your own mini shelf art.

### 3. DON'T be too stuffy

In the living room of a cosy country retreat (opposite), a mix of blue and white ceramic jars and whimsical objects have been tucked in among the books on the shelves. Framed illustrations hung in front of the shelves make the display look more interesting.

A library should feel well loved. Relaxing the angles of books, making them higgledy-piggledy, immediately creates a calmer, more casual feel. It also looks as if you have read every book – always a win-win.

Incorporating smaller frames along the shelves rather than on the walls also helps to break up rows of books beautifully.

A collection of old plates (above left) looks better lining the shelves of an antique French fruitwood dresser than hidden away, forgotten about, in a cupboard.

In one of our top-floor duplex suites at One Denman Place in London (above right), a cosy nook has been created for whiling away the hours, reading or writing. The walls are lined in my 'Ozone' fabric for Christopher Farr Cloth, which contrasts with a colourful collection of books, arranged to face in different directions to add interest.

# HOW TO HANG ART TO TELL A STORY

If a picture can tell a thousand words, then an interestingly framed one shouts volumes. Anything can be elevated – pages from a children's picture book, a collection of plastic insects, a favourite handkerchief, a deck of playing cards or pieces of fabric – into admirable works of art.

## 1. DO be inventive

Framing makes you look at things with fresh eyes – and often, the stranger the artwork, the more inventive the frame. In the past, I have created frames from old mobile phone cases and printing press letters to old twine, leather belt buckles, the front of a kennel and an oar from a boat.

For a portrait of Brumus (top right), one of my family's beloved Cavalier King Charles Spaniels (whose name we took for the restaurant at the Haymarket Hotel, the frame has been creatively made from the labels of dog food tins.

## 2. DON'T be scared of adding bold colours

An easy and inexpensive way to freshen up a neutral room is by adding colour through paintings, collages and frames. In this corner of a charming country sitting room (opposite, left), four vividly printed handkerchiefs by Peter Adler are imaginatively framed to add life and impact to the white walls.

I have framed beautifully illustrated pages from books of fairy tales (opposite, right), and a collection of antique iron keys against the vibrantly patterned background to look fresh and contemporary (bottom right).

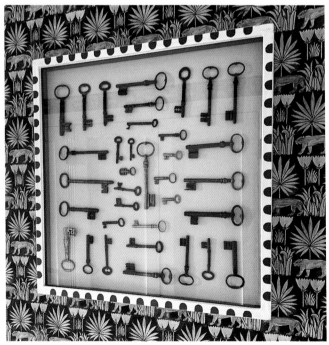

### 3. DO create collections and frame them together

Rather than hanging only conventional prints or paintings, why not create your own collection of favourite or interesting objects? When grouped together and cleverly framed, this creates a unique feature for any wall.

At Crosby Street Hotel (above), plastic insects, framed in an interesting and witty way, have been hung above a mother- of-pearl inlaid chest of drawers, next to a headboard upholstered in a fabric by Andrew Martin and a cushion by Bennison. Meanwhile, at Charlotte Street Hotel (left), we made this eye-catching artwork using a collection of fabric butterflies, bought inexpensively, to fill a large Perspex frame.

### 4. DON'T hang artworks too high or too low

It is important to hang paintings at the height of the viewer's eyes – not too tall and not too low. Approximately 170 cm (70 in) from the floor to

the middle of the art piece is a good average
to work with (bottom right).

### 5. DO get creative with framing

Framing is important – I like to frame things in
such a way that the illustration looks more striking
and stands its ground in a room. If a piece you love
is too small for the wall, consider reframing it with
a larger mount. A small picture in a large frame
looks dramatic and calls for attention.

Different framing ideas, as used in a corner
area of the bar at Ham Yard Hotel (top right),
lend energy and colour to the space – here,
illustrations of the four queens (Queen Elizabeth
II, Queen Elizabeth I, Queen Victoria and
Mary, Queen of Scots) sit above the sofa and
photography of culinary objects by Simon Brown
above a hand-painted chest displaying lamps
custom-made in neon Perspex with Ikat shades.

### 6. DO hang pieces together

Hanging artworks together is often more
effective than using one on each wall, where they
can look lost. It is also interesting to group items
by technique or topic, such as botanical prints or
a watercolour series.

### 7. DO use alternative methods

If you are reluctant to make permanent changes
to a wall, you can always lean a picture against it
or use a picture shelf to create an ever-changing
display of artworks. Even two or three pictures
leaning on a mantelpiece with other objects can
look great – and you can change them as often as
you wish.

# HOW TO USE FOUND FABRICS

I often talk about my love of textiles and how important it is to bring together the old and new in interior design. Found fabrics really capture my love of craft, of telling a story and paying homage to the past in new and exciting ways. However, using found fabrics comes with a few challenges. Over the years, I have learnt crafty tips and tricks for working with antique and found textiles:

## 1. DO use the fabric as your starting point

When you have a fabric that you love and want to bring to life in a scheme, it's always a good idea to pick colours from the textile itself. Think of the fabric as the blueprint for the rest of the space and grow the identity from there. Carefully building on these colours will help to create a cohesive and balanced room.

## 2. DON'T be afraid to make a statement

Found fabrics come in many forms, depending on origin, technique or era. Often, they feature delicate and pretty designs, but sometimes you might be lucky enough to find a punchy and powerful design, like this traditional Mexican Otomi embroidery (left). This fabric makes such a statement that the rest of the scheme doesn't require too much detail to feel exciting.

feel more unique. Play into the imperfect by using a combination of similar fabrics. Kilim rugs are one of my favourite fabrics to collect – one afternoon, while browsing my design library, I realised I had a small collection of hot pink and orange pieces. I had just enough to cover my dining chairs at home (see page 138), so they went straight off to the upholsterer with the help of Andrew Martin. It doesn't matter that they are all slightly different, the mix-and-match mood lends intrigue.

### 5. DO pay homage to your fabric

Play into the origins of your antique textiles to create a scheme that tells a story. A beautiful antique needlepoint on the ottoman (see page 139) is wonderfully traditional and tells a tale of age-old craft techniques.

In the library at The Soho Hotel, two hand-embroidered throws found in the shop at the American Folk Art Museum in

### 3. DO create a patchwork

If you have a small piece of fabric but you are desperate to use it on a larger piece of furniture, I recommend pairing it with a strong plain wool or linen that complements the original textile. I always place the lovely antique fabric, crewelwork or tapestry that I'm using on the front of a chair, and then cover the back and outer sides of the chair in a complementary plain fabric.

### 4. DON'T shy away from mixing and matching

The joy and beauty of using found or vintage fabrics is that their imperfections make them

# Sometimes a textile is so special that you just have to use it

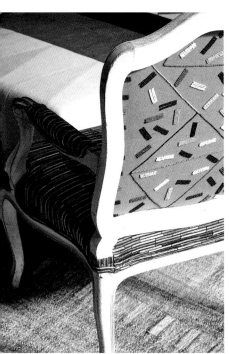

New York have been used to transform two wing chairs (top left). I have always been drawn to folk art and craft but mixing these throws with Clementine Oliver wools created a more contemporary feel.

A small detail can provide the lyrical element that brings a whole room to life. Look for unusual fabrics with a design or detail that captures your imagination – these will be the things people remember in a room.

## 6. DON'T overlook the potential for wear and tear

Using antique textiles often means the fabric might be fragile. There could be delicate embroidery or embellishment, or the textile itself may have lost its lustre over time. The more delicate the fabric, the more important it is to use it in a location which will get less wear and tear. My trick is to use more intricate fabrics on accent chairs in spaces where people are only passing through – or on the back of a chair where it can last longer (bottom left).

## 7. DO be prepared to break the rules

I know how tempting it is to store your found textiles so they're safe from harm, but I have always been one to throw out the rule book – sometimes a textile is so special that you just have to use it! I have been known to use pieces like the most intricately embroidered Kantha cloths in the most unlikely places, such as on an ottoman or end-of-bed footstool. Another trick here is to use large Perspex trays on top of the ottomans to help preserve these most precious pieces.

# FIRESIDE TALES

**Fireplaces are one of our favourite focal points in a room. While they are functional, they also provide the bones for a space, providing a special focal point and playing to the many textures of a space.**

From beautifully carved, ornate stone to antique wooden mantles saved from reclamation yards, fireplaces always lend gravitas to the atmosphere of a room.  Here are some tips and tricks for fireplaces:

### 1. DO use antiques
Sitting by the fireside is a centuries-old tradition – there is something romantic and nostalgic about taking a seat beside a fire with a good book or a glass of wine. Using a special antique

fireplace is guaranteed to bring a beautiful, aged quality to a room.

There is an authenticity to a fireplace, like this one at Charlotte Street Hotel (opposite) provides, with its slightly charred and beautifully weathered stone mantel.

This fireplace at Covent Garden Hotel (above) has a wonderfully ornate stone face and wooden surround. The play between the wood panelling and the carved stone adds to the many layers of history in this space. (You would never know we added all the wood panelling and fireplace in this room – a design secret.)

There is something romantic
and nostalgic about taking
a seat beside a fire

## 2. DO accessorise

If you have a simple fireplace, a great way to create an interesting focal point in the room is by dressing it up, accessorising it with collections.

The little hearth in a country house kitchen (see page 144) has a robust collection of antique charges on a plate rack above it to help draw the eye to this corner of the room. On the mantle, a fun collection of glass vases and candlesticks from William Yeoward reflect the light coming into the room.

A lovely antique French fireplace in this cosy drawing room (opposite, bottom) has been dressed up with wooden sculptures, a little model boat and logs in the cubby at the bottom. These elements are all simple but come together to create a curated feel.

Alternatively, a fireplace can be ablaze with a floral cluster (see page 145) rather than a typical roaring fire. If your fireplace isn't used often, or is predominantly decorative, then popping in fun pieces such as this painted bouquet brings life to the dead space within the fireplace.

## 3. DON'T be afraid to use smoke and mirrors

If you don't have a fireplace in your home, don't let that stop you – build out a section of your wall to allow for the inside of a fireplace, then a 'faux' fireplace can immediately feel as though it has always been there. Painting the back of the fireplace black, and sometimes adding a faux fire, can work wonders for creating the feeling of a very real and usable fireplace.

### 4. DO make it your focal point

Creating symmetrical furniture layouts around a fireplace makes it the centre of attention in a room. After all, home is where the hearth is.

### 5. DON'T forget to listen to the room

It is so important when dressing or designing any room to have a chat with it first. What does the room need? What is the energy and feel of the space? This suite at The Whitby Hotel (opposite) is so wonderfully traditional, it almost needed a more masculine and geometric fireplace to stop the room from becoming overly fussy. It's all about striking the right balance.

### 6. DO play with height

When you have high ceilings in a room, fireplaces with tall pediments above are a must. This fireplace in the lobby at Charlotte Street Hotel (top right) is simple and sophisticated, with a feeling of humble grandeur. It makes the room feel finished while drawing the eye upwards to appreciate the height of the space.

# CREATING A KIT KEMP HEADBOARD

**1. DON'T hold back**

Find a fabric you love and go for it – you might be making the headboard the focal point of a room, but it's actually a relatively small area in relation to the rest of the space, so don't be afraid to use something bold.

Choosing a fun print or weave with multiple colours can also help to guide a room's colour scheme. For example, if the headboard fabric is made up of blues, greens and yellows, you could then use blue on the walls, another patterned fabric with a complementary green for the curtains, and a combination of blues and yellows for the valance.

A headboard is also the one upholstery item that requires the least meterage of fabric – so if you've fallen in love with something really special, use it on the headboard and pair it with a more economical plain or striped linen for curtains to help even out your budget.

**Oversized headboards have become one of the Kit Kemp Design Studio's most iconic and recognisable design features. They play into all the things I love to accentuate in a room – our headboards are bold, striking and memorable.**

Elevating the humble headboard to create maximum impact in a room not only provides a lovely way for showcasing the detail of a fabric's beautiful embroidery, appliqué, collage or beadwork, but it is also the perfect opportunity to create something truly personal and unique for your bedroom.

Here are some tricks of the trade for creating your own headboard centrepiece:

## 2. DO think about the shape

When choosing a fabric, consider which headboard shape lends itself best to the design and pattern repeat of the fabric.

With a geometric pattern or stripe you may want to accentuate the vertical with a more upright, elongated shape; a floral motif might be best complemented with a softer, more feminine edge. Of course, there are no rules, so play around and mix things up – a floral fabric used on a more streamlined shape can feel chic and modern; the curves of a headboard might echo the curves of an overscaled botanical print.

## 3. DON'T forget the detail

I'm always looking for ways to layer extra accents into a room – here are some examples for headboards:

### Studding

Metal upholstery studs are a great way to help define the headboard edge like a frame. I use a wide variety of sizes and finishes – I'm particularly fond of large, widely spaced, nickel studs because this feels really strong and contemporary.

### Piping

Contrast piping is a favourite upholstery design detail which works equally well framing the front edge of a headboard as it does on a chair

or cushion. Leather and wool piping also lends additional colour and texture; vertical piping within a headboard's design can also be effective for separating fabrics if you are combining patterns with plains.

**Contrast depth**
Upholstering the depth of a headboard in a contrast fabric is another clever detail (above). It outlines the headboard and lifts it from the wall, making it really pop. It works best in a plain, picked out from one of the colours in the main headboard fabric, ideally contrasted with the wall colour.

**4. DO mix and match**
Using a combination of fabrics and textures is a great trick for adding an extra layer of detail to a scheme. Using a smaller scale print or plain as a border, paired with a larger print as the main headboard fabric, lends depth and interest. Pair plains to create a dynamic colour blocking effect, which looks especially strong against a patterned wall.

### 5. DON'T be put off if a fabric is not wide enough

One of my great loves is sourcing antique textiles on my travels because they so often inspire my designs. While they look beautiful hung in decorative frames, I also can't resist using them for upholstery. Very often, the fragments and panels I source are not wide enough to cover a headboard, so I pair them with a complementary fabric to cover the full width.

At the Knightsbridge Hotel, I used an old Designers Guild blanket with two drops of orange moon tweed along either side to make up the full width (see page 150).

### 6. DO create a work of art

A headboard can also provide the perfect canvas for storytelling – it infuses further narrative into a room, whether that be with the whimsy of Goddess Aurora flying through the sky, surrounded by her cherubs (opposite, bottom) or a simple, subtle embellishment of an existing pattern. On a headboard upholstered in Blithfield's 'Oakleaves' fabric, taken from its Peggy Angus collection, the veins of some of the leaves, and the petals of flowers chosen at random, have been hand-embroidered in accents of vibrant red, yellow and green by Fine Cell Work (above).

In this bedroom (above), I started with 'Tasha's Trip' on the curtains. With my design team, we enlarged and deconstructed the flower detail, creating a bespoke beaded collage design to be stitched onto the boiled wool upholstering the headboard. Appliqué like this allows me to play with scale and texture, as well as adding an individual, unexpected touch that cleverly ties the whole room together.

# LIGHTING UP A ROOM

**While lighting is functional, there is no reason why it can't also be a talking point.**

Here are some thoughts on lighting up a room:

### 1. DO make a lighting plan

Before you think about investing in lamps and light fittings, make sure you really understand the room, considering the functions and activities that will take place there. Will you be eating, reading, relaxing or working?

'shh design secrets'

Really gauge what type of lighting you will need for these tasks. Never rely on guesswork – I recommend drawing a simple scale plan of the room (opposite), including key features such as windows, doors and a rough furniture layout, then highlight the areas you want to light up and the types of lighting you think will be most useful.

Kitchens require more concentrated and direct lighting for cooking. For a top-floor apartment in Chelsea (overleaf, top right), discreet strips of LED lighting recessed and hidden beneath wall cabinets prove a fantastic way for illuminating the work surfaces. If you have a larger kitchen with an island, add a colourful collection of pendant lights above it (right).

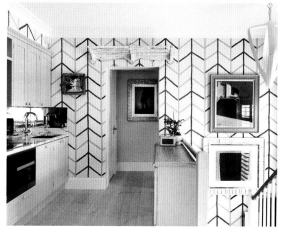

## 2. DON'T overdo it with spotlights

I try to avoid using spotlights where possible, especially in rooms such as living rooms, libraries, and bedrooms because these spaces are meant to be warm and inviting. I have created low-level lighting with table lamps, an illuminated ladder and picture wall lights (see previous page, top right).

Although spotlights can be overbearing and garish, and ruin the look of a ceiling, don't abandon them completely. Only use them where necessary and put them on a dimmer switch so you can soften or brighten

the glow. They also work well positioned just in front of, or inside, a bedroom or dressing room wardrobe so you can see everything inside. Uplighters in the corner of a room can often help make a space feel bigger. An uplighter behind a sculpture or table in a corner can create a real focal point by highlighting the object and creating interesting shadows that lead your eye further into the space.

## 3. DO make a statement

One of the most frequently used light features is the chandelier, but I like to find more modern alternatives to the old-fashioned crystal

chandeliers, replicating the same grandeur and drama only in a modern setting, like this contemporary blue chandelier (above left).

I have recently collaborated with lighting company Porta Romana, to design a series of mobile pendants, and floor and table lights in combinations of porcelain plaster and twine. When switched on, the porcelain gives out a soft warm glow (opposite, top).

**4. DON'T forget the importance of bathroom lighting**

So many people rely on a single central light fitting in bathrooms, but overhead lighting alone can cast shadows, which can be frustrating when you are trying to apply makeup or shaving. Proper task lighting is important – placing strategic spotlights by the entrance and above the shower is key. The best lighting for when standing in front of the mirror is to position wall lights either side. Favourites include the pillar lights from Original BTC as these give an even and flattering light. In the striking monochromatic bathroom that I recently designed for C.P Hart (left, middle and bottom), above the freestanding gunmetal-blue bath, a bull's-eye infinity mirror acts as an imaginary window, adding depth and starlight beyond the room. I added a dash of textured red to the space with Balineum's coral-shaped lights either side of the bath and Porta Romana's plaster-finished Bronte lights by the mirror.

Courtesy lights can also be useful for nighttime as they can be set on a sensor, turning on automatically to provide a gentle dim glow.

**5. DO consider the detailing in lighting**

Don't forget about bookshelves and shadow gaps – recessed LED strip lights under shelving makes a library space come alive. Books should be celebrated, never forgotten.

Another detail which is VERY important to remember is to use a 5 AMP plug socket – I know electrics can seem daunting and confusing, but 5 AMP plug circuits are a lifesaver. In simple terms, you can plug in all your standing and table lamps and have them all connected to one switch at the door. It saves so much time going round the room turning lamps off individually.

It is amazing how the power
of colour can influence your mood
and spice up your life

# COLOUR MAKES YOU HAPPY

How To Create A Bloomsbury Inspired Interior
Under The Yellow Sun | Spring Greens
If Life Gives You Lemons

# HOW TO CREATE A BLOOMSBURY INSPIRED INTERIOR

It's no secret that I have long been inspired by the work and creativity of the Bloomsbury Group, a set of artists and intellectuals, including Vanessa Bell and Duncan Grant, who lived and worked in Bloomsbury in Central London during the early 20th century. The group believed in creativity, innovation and beauty, but it is their sense of fun and freedom that I am most drawn to.

Charlotte Street Hotel (above) sits in the heart of Bloomsbury and the interiors for the hotel make specific reference to the Bloomsbury Group. There is much to learn from this fascinating group of artists – here are some ideas for how to create a Bloomsbury interior of your own:

### Inspirational Places:
### Charleston and Duncan Grant's Studio

When creating your own Bloomsbury-inspired interior, there is no better way to seek inspiration than by visiting the Charleston farmhouse near Lewes, in East Sussex, England, where the group's interior style can be most distinctly seen. Vanessa Bell, with artists Duncan Grant and Roger Fry, wanted art to be democratic and thought that furniture, ceramics and textiles should be given as much attention as fine art. So here they filled the home they shared with beautiful things and painted every surface (top and middle).

*Top and middle: Duncan Grant's studio (photograph by Tony Tree); bottom: Kit at the front door of Charleston (photograph by Craig Markham)*

Another place from which to draw Bloomsbury inspiration is Monk's House, also in East Sussex (right), where the spirit of not only Virginia Woolf, who lived here with her husband Leonard, but also of the Bloomsbury Group and the many artists, writers and thinkers who visited, fills the rooms.

## Colour palette

The Bloomsbury Group truly loved colour. Their interiors and paintings were a riot of dusky blues, artichoke greens, damask rose, burnt orange and aubergine. It is a totally unique colour palette that can be both moody and uplifting. Annie Sloan, the chalk paint specialist, has collaborated with the Charleston Trust to create a unique range of paint colours inspired by these distinctive hues.

In the Drawing Room and Library at Charlotte Street Hotel, the curtains have been made up in Duncan Grant's 'Queen Mary' fabric (below right), which was intended for use in the First Class Lounge aboard the RMS *Queen Mary* ocean liner in 1935. This is available from Charleston's shop.

Sydney-based fabric house EDIT offers a selection of incredibly colourful and vibrant fabrics which take the Bloomsbury aesthetic into the 21st century. I have used EDIT's 'Harlequin' fabric on occasional chairs at Charlotte Street Hotel in both the Library (right), positioned below a painting by Roger Fry, and the Drawing Room (below).

I have also used EDIT's 'Vanessa Bloom' – named after Vanessa Bell – on a comfortable fireside armchair in the Drawing Room (above left). This fabric evokes the spirit of the Bloomsbury Group with its rich, painterly forest green, pink and blue florals.

*Opposite, bottom right: Charlotte Street Hotel, Bloomsbury-inspired lamp base; opposite, bottom left: fireplace at Charleston Farmhouse*

**Design details**
A great way to update a room is to paint the furniture in it. The Bloomsbury Group loved breathing new, colourful and witty life into everyday items by painting them with decorative motifs and geometric patterns.

At Charlotte Street Hotel, there is a small desk that was hand-painted by The Omega Workshop (opposite, top left), over which hang paintings by Duncan Grant (left) and Vanessa Bell (right). The Omega Workshop was founded by Roger Fry in Bloomsbury's Fitzroy Square in 1913, with

the aim of selling furniture, fabrics and household accessories designed and made by the Bloomsbury Group's unconventional group of artists. They had an eclectic set of influences, where Cubist design would sit next to Italian frescoes and neoclassical pieces rest against English Arts & Crafts designs.

In the same way, be inspired in your own home by mixing different styles and eras, displaying things you find both useful *and* beautiful, but most importantly things that you really love.

In the Library at Charlotte Street Hotel (above right), Vanessa Bell's painted panels set the Bloomsbury mood, teamed here with a wing chair covered in a modern Bloomsbury-inspired fabric.

# UNDER THE YELLOW SUN

**Sunshine isn't always guaranteed in London, where my design studio is based, so I like to add a touch of yellow to brighten up our design schemes.**

At Covent Garden Hotel (above), I lined the walls with my 'Willow' fabric for Christopher Farr Cloth in Lemon (one of the most popular colourways) to amplify the light and add depth to the walls.

This creates a striking contrast with the dark bespoke headboard, featuring appliquéd falling leaves in autumnal shades of golden yellow. This tactile detailing reflects the bold yellow on the curtains and walls, creating a unified whole.

In the Library at Number Sixteen (above),
zesty pops of yellow on the furniture, wallpaper
and upholstery make the room feel summery
and bright.

Yellow can also be used to create a romantic scheme. In Room 417
at Covent Garden Hotel (above and opposite), I covered the traditional
corona in a Lee Jofa floral fabric on the outer side and contrasted
it with a lining in a soft yellow print by Tissus d'Hélène. These pastel
tones, complemented by pale pink walls and cushions embroidered in
my Large Susani design for Chelsea Textiles in contemporary colours,
create a dreamy mood in an otherwise classic setting.

In the Drawing Room of the Oak Leaf Suite at Ham Yard Hotel (above), I used warm and sunny yellow tones – walls lined in yellow linen, hung with artworks by Joe Tilson and Michael Vaughan, are punctuated with flashes of bright yellow and a sofa by the window covered in my 'Woven Ribbon' fabric for Christopher Farr Cloth, piped in yellow leather.

# SPRING GREENS

**Green is the colour of life, hope, energy and nature, so I often use it to breathe fresh air into a room.**

In The Whitby Hotel's Terrace Suite 1402 (above and opposite), the walls of the Drawing Room are papered in my 'Friendly Folk' design, featuring a chalky white background with soft green figures. The windows are framed in the same design, but in reverse on a leafy green linen with two matching tub chairs in front.

There are hints of green too in the comfy armchair and cushions covered in my 'Hedgerow' design (opposite). I love the way little jewels of pink burst from the linen like spring flowers, making you quite forget Manhattan's concrete jungle outside.

The Grisaille
painting adds depth
to the scheme

In the Terrace Suite at Ham Yard Hotel (above and opposite, left), Natasha Hulse has intricately appliquéd one of our signature headboards with an elaborate floral design. The three-dimensional quality of her work gives the room depth and breaks the boundary between indoors and outdoors. This teams perfectly with Tobias and the Angel's fabric in Olive, which is used for the curtains, and my 'Rain Shadow' cushions for Fine Cell Work on the bed.

The leafy block-printed linen curtains have been finished with a knotted lime-green trim down the leading edge (above).

A deep garden-green floral fabric from Christopher Farr Cloth's 'Raoul Dufy' Collection upholstering the tall, curving headboard (above), set against the subtly patterned 'Isabena' fabric by Nina Campbell on the walls at Number Sixteen is a wonderful example of balancing greens and blues to harmonious effect.

In subtle contrast, the linen of the curtains made in my 'Travelling Light' fabric drapes beautifully to the floor, its white background looking fresh against the leafy view of the gardens outside and the handsome Handle chair and the West Timber Tub chairs covered in green leather with stitched white piping (opposite).

# Getting the texture and the tone right is important

At Crosby Street Hotel (right), I have used my 'Ozone' fabric for Christopher Farr Cloth in Green on the headboard and my 'Mud Print' design on the walls to create a bright and airy scheme which feels like spring.

In the drawing room of this one-bedroom suite (above, opposite top and overleaf), with walls upholstered in an orange Casamance fabric, I used my 'Friendly Folk' design in Melon Orange on both the curtains and cushions, and in Basil Green on the armchairs. Combined with Lewis & Wood's 'Tribal' fabric in Limpopo Green on the sofas, this playful reverse colour combination adds freshness to the warm room. A solid orange trim on both the curtains and cushions also helps to frame the fabric, creating a sense of harmony and nature in this spacious suite.

'Friendly Folk' is also used on the walls (and on the back side of the adjoining doors) in the bedroom, combined with a colour-blocked, mossy green wool on the headboard (above).

My fabric 'Loom Weave' for Christopher Farr Cloth adds texture to the little tub chairs positioned by the fireplace (left). Orange piping and a navy leather tassel add a contrasting finishing touch.

# IF LIFE GIVES YOU LEMONS

**Lemon-yellow, lime-green and tangerine-orange are staple hues in the colour palette I use in both my fabric and wallpaper collections, and in the spaces I design. We all need some brightness in our lives – here are some favourite citrus-themed schemes.**

This striking bedroom interior at Covent Garden Hotel (above and opposite) colourfully showcases my 'One Way' fabric for Christopher Farr Cloth, used here in Lemon on the curtains. I love the large scale of this print – the simple vertical design adds height to the space and its white ground lends a crisp backdrop.

# Mirrors reflect light in the narrow room

Fanny Shorter's 'Margo' fabric in Lemon makes the headboard a vibrant focal point in this sunny scheme (above) The sharp plain yellow fabric used to make up the outside quarter edge of the bed cushions is a great trick for balancing colour in a scheme. The mirrors opposite the window also cleverly reflect light around the room, making it feel bigger and brighter.

I was immediately drawn to the painterly quality of Jim Thompson's playful 'Garden Party' in Orangerie, which I've used here on the headboard (opposite). It also inspired the upscaled motif of leafy oranges, which have been appliquéd onto felted wool for the bed cushions.

In contrast, having the same fabric for the bed cushions shows how this joyful design can be equally effective when used on a smaller scale (above).

How to add that 'wow' factor
to your interiors

# TOP TIPS

# TIPS FOR PLAYING WITH
# PICTORIAL PATTERNS

I love using bold patterns in my work, from traditional florals and smart stripes to modern, graphic designs. The bolder, the better – especially patterns with motif-heavy repeats that tell a story. However, these designs are often the hardest to use. You must be brave and bold when working with busy patterns, but also know when to pare it back. Here are my four tips for using complex pictorial patterns.

### 1. Tone It Down

A way to bring calm to the chaos of working with busy fabrics or wallpapers is to use the patterns in softer, more natural colours.

In this room at Crosby Street Hotel (opposite), the intriguing mural wallpaper transports you to the wonderful world of 'Emily's Garden'. In the interior scheme, I used a combination of soft plain upholstery fabrics to create balance and calm in the room, but also to ensure that the intricate storytelling of the wallpaper remained the star of the show. A splash of pattern on the mannequin and bed cushions provided a final flourish of detail.

### 2. Fire it up

In complete contrast, this room at The Whitby Hotel (above) emphasises a feast of colour in the bold and rich design used for the headboard. This wonderful fabric, inspired by the art of Asafo flags, is one of my favourites from Raoul Textiles.

To make the most of the design, the entire scheme is alive with colour and detail. For the curtains, I used my 'Tea Leaf' design with its cascading orange vines, bringing in another pattern but mixing the scales to create

stability. On the walls, I used a plain fabric so as not to fight the statement headboard, but the fiery hue makes it exciting. By playing into the hot and bold tones of the fabric, I have created a space where this fun textile feels at home and not at odds with the space.

### 3. Continue the narrative
In the Indigo Room at The Soho Hotel (above), the wallpaper reminded me of a lost and forgotten city. Rather than shy away from the rich pattern provided by the wallpaper, I overlaid a strong artwork that played further into the story. It evokes a sense of the travellers in the painting discovering the landscape in the wallpaper beyond.

### 4. Opposites attract
In Room 109 at Charlotte Street Hotel (opposite), a landscape mural made especially for the room, wraps spellbindingly around the length and breadth of the room's double-height, 4 m (13 ft) high walls. I paired the mural with curtains in my large, repeat graphic fabric 'One Way' to create an interesting contrast with the romantic narrative of the 'Tall Trees' wallpaper. Don't be afraid to use geometric prints with more painterly designs – opposites definitely attract, and the unexpected combination of patterns can create a modern and fresh twist.

# HOW TO DRESS YOUR TABLE

**While I am best known for my interiors, I also love to dress tables with glorious decorations and tasty nibbles. Our top tips for dressing a table are:**

**1.** Just like an interior, you can create a dramatic look on a table if the colours of the decoration work in harmony with the room. Using seasonal flowers, with a just-picked-from-the-garden feel, always adds charm and freshness.

**2.** Small flower arrangements in jam jars, pots or bud vases work best when you want to fit other items around them on the table.

194

**3.** Avoid high floral arrangements so guests can speak to one another across the table.

**4.** Use foliage and fresh fruit to create a dramatic look of abundancy, perhaps laying multiple bowls of pomegranates, leafy clementines, lemons and limes, cherries, grapes or redcurrants along the table. This is an inexpensive way of adding decoration with the bonus of being able to eat them at the same time. Dried fruits, cinnamon sticks, oranges studded with cloves and sugar-dusted fruits also add a festive scented touch.

**5**. When decorating a display table, using height can create great impact. Play with a variety of handmade wooden chopping boards laden with whatever you fancy, from

charcuterie and cheeses to cakes, chocolates or fruits, elevating some of the arrangement by placing cake stands on top of wooden logs for a rustic look (bottom left).

**6.** Create arrangements with an unexpected twist – rather than flowers, line the table with terracotta pots filled with fragrant herbs, such as rosemary, thyme, mint, oregano and lemon verbena (opposite, bottom left).

**7.** Candles are essential for creating a warm, inviting atmosphere, night and day. Always place tealights in holders to avoid them burning through to the table's surface (opposite, bottom right). You can use anything from crystal glasses to mismatched vintage teacups – let your imagination run wild. Hurricane lamps at different heights work well at any time of the day, while at night candelabra with elegant tapered candles add a dramatic and romantic touch (just be sure that the candelabra stem raises the candles above eye level).

# A RECIPE FOR DESIGNING A RUG

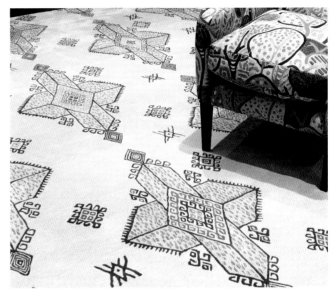

Choosing a rug for your room is a careful balancing act. It should be a statement piece, breathing extra colour and life into the space, but you also need to ensure that it does not fight with the myriad of textures under which it sits.

I love using vintage or antique rugs, but I have discovered that designing my own area rug for a space really lends a bespoke touch to a room.

### 1. Pattern

I tend to choose the most graphic and punchy fabric in a room's design scheme as inspiration for a rug, because this helps to create a thread between it and the other materials in the room, as well as ensuring the rug has weight and presence.

For example, in the Library at The Soho Hotel (opposite, top left), the classic herringbone pattern of my 'By Way' design for Wilton Carpets, woven in a bright colour combination, works perfectly with the vibrant design of my 'Ikat Weave' used on the sofa.

'Domino', another carpet I designed for Wilton Carpets, was inspired by my love for Turkish rugs (opposite, bottom right). I reimagined an existing design into something original by developing a subtle diamond repeat and then changing the colour of the individual blocks within the overall design. When looking at the design closely, you barely notice the overall repeat – instead your eye is drawn to the little geometric blocks – and it is only when you stand back that the larger diamond pattern is revealed.

Above, I collaborated with Pierre Frey to match a rug with the fabric.

### The Recipe

Within my design process, the rug tends to be one of the last things I think about. Once I have the scheme together, and I have a strong idea of its tones and the story, then the rug can come to life.

One of my favourite tricks is to base my rug on one of the fabrics in the scheme. This way, I am at an advantage with several pieces of knowledge: the colours work well together, the balance of the design works, and the rug will undoubtedly harmonise with the scheme.

Here is my recipe for the careful mixing of ingredients that will make your rug come to life:

**199**

This is a sneak peek of one of our new rug designs for the Massachusetts-based designer Annie Selke, a powerhouse in textile and rug design in the USA (right). Together, we are designing a collection of rugs and bed linens for the home, where bold, vibrant colour will be at play.

## 2. Colour play

Getting the colours right ensures a rug doesn't fight with the rest of the space. When designing the rug in Crosby Street Hotel's Drawing Room, I wanted to create an oversized version of the collaged wing chairs (below left).

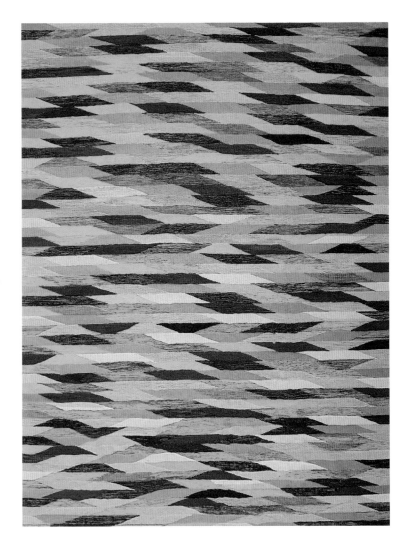

I spent a long time matching the rug poms to the wools used to create the chair, setting the base of the rug in a darker tone, rather than the white of the upholstery, because it's a cosy space and having something moodier felt right.

In the event space at Crosby Street Hotel, this geometric rug was designed to reflect the vibrancy of Peter Rocklin's hyperrealistic paintings and the kitsch ice-lolly rocket light by Andrew Martin (opposite, bottom right).

### 3. Texture

In all elements of my design work, texture is key. It creates depth and intrigue, which is especially important for a rug. Experiment with mixing both tufted and knotted techniques – the differentiation in texture can also serve to break up an intricate design.

For example, another rug I designed (above left and right) helped to create a thread between the colours of the textile covering an end-of-bed stool with the suite's adjoining drawing room – a tight knotted background recreates the linen effect of the fabric, while the tufting technique replicates the elevated texture of the colourful, graphic woven design.

# THE ART OF TEXTURE

**I could talk about the importance of texture with my design team all day. To us, the best interiors marry different textures and unexpected details within the scheme.**

When choosing the textures and colour palette, I always consider the natural light within a room first. If it is a cold, indirect light, layers of textures on felt embroidery and patterned fabrics make a room feel warm. In a sunny room with good light, a darker colour on the walls works well, contrasted with brighter fabrics on the upholstery. Without texture, interiors can look flat and cold, so layering rough with smooth, cosy with sleek, embellished or carved with clean and plain is one of the most important parts of my design process (opposite and below). This tactility and attention to detail captures, satisfies, and inspires all the senses.

I gravitate towards fabrics that are rich with natural imperfections and texture within the weave – it's an easy and immediate way to imbue a

space with understated luxury. A blend of linens and wools, weaves and prints lend depth within a room as the raised surfaces reflect light and create shadows.

Fabric walling has become one of my hallmarks (opposite, top left). I like using linen because it is at once comfortable yet effortlessly chic, cocooning – absorbing sound and adding warmth – yet tailored and hard-wearing.

In the Drawing Room at Ham Yard Hotel (opposite, above right and below right), textures abound. Sofas upholstered in embroidered crewelwork fabric and a colourful patchwork printed cotton, a decoratively painted antique Swedish armoire and a Breon O'Casey rug keep company with an Eileen Cooper painting and a burnt wood and slate coffee table by Tom Stogdon. Combined together, this creates an interesting and layered living space.

# HOW TO USE COLOUR IN DESIGN

My designs always play with a collage of colour, pattern and texture. It is a style best described as carefree and colourful – when working in an uncompromising city landscape, I like to return to a room filled with light and colour because it makes me happy. Below are my top five tips on how to use colour in design:

### 1. Think of colour in terms of shades

When working out which colours will work together, look at the different shades and tones. For example, if you crack open a watermelon, you see red and green. However, look more closely and you will see different shades, from watery white, shell-pink and yellow grey to the dark black of the pips. I look to the way these colours seamlessly blend from one to the other to learn how to create harmonious colour palettes.

### 2. Not everything in a room should zing with colour

Balance and scale are an important part of the equation. I look at the plans of a room as a whole, and then create a sequence of spaces so that a calm area leads into a vivid colourscape (above). I like spaces to tell a story and lift the imagination as I travel through them.

### 3. Choose a specific palette to suit the room

I look at the aspect of a room and decide how I want it to feel. If it is gloomy, with no

direct sunlight, a dark navy-blue wall will seem uninviting and heavy, so a more reflective, lighter tone of blue with a hint of warmth will work better. I can then add touches of dark navy to the piping of a chair or as a trim to the leading edge of a curtain to still get the feel of the shade without overwhelming a space that lacks light.

Conversely, in a sunny room with good light, I can use denim on the walls with a contrasting colour for the curtains, such as a patterned fabric with a bright yellow trim, which will please the eye (left).

## 4. Be inspired by nature

I often look to nature for ideas of colour palettes that work harmoniously together, such as the natural hues of ochre, terracotta, sienna or indigo. From a base of these organic tones, I can create different moods with various colour and pattern combinations.

## 5. Throw in a neutral

I love all colours, but there always needs to be a neutral thrown in to give the room some breathing space. It is important to be bold, not frantic (below left).

Here's one we made earlier.
Be creative and enjoy the process!

# CREATIVITY AT HOME

Painted Frames At Home | Rebecca's Paper Puzzles

Mimi's Shell Mirror | Stella's Potato Block

Polly's Patchwork Lampshade | Melissa's Treasure Box

Minnie's Embroidered Magical Micro Garden | Ruby's Collage

Appliqué At Home | Appliqué Cushion

Cristina's Candlesticks

# PAINTED FRAMES AT HOME

When it comes to artwork, I love a wonderful one-off frame. Throughout our hotels you will spot thousands of different ways to frame a piece of art, from a simple Perspex box, to driftwood, to painted simply in a wacky form. Our clever framer Marcus Wells has reinvented the art of framing, making the frame an art form in itself.

It is important for a frame to work in harmony with the artwork. Our talented framer says that 'Pictures always have clues in them – a colour, a detail, a texture – which spark ideas'.

I like to frame things in such a way that the artwork looks more striking and stands its ground in a room.

In my schemes, art isn't confined to expensive paintings – I like to play with still lifes bought for almost nothing at a vintage fair, exotic postcards, illustrations from books, museum posters or found textiles (opposite and below left). Equally, our frames are not only gilded – they are patterned, painted, embellished with mother-or-pearl or mirror, framed within a frame (below right) or wittily decorated with buttons, dominoes or playing cards.

When designing a frame, for example, for a postcard of an abstract painting by Carrie Goldsmith, with green and blue hues as well as hints of ochre (overleaf, bottom), I started with an old frame that was no longer in use, but you could also look online for an inexpensive wooden frame as an alternative. For this project, I used acrylic paints, unlike a professional framer who would use gesso and wax to create their masterpiece.

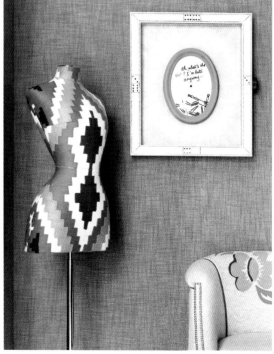

Carrying the painting's curvaceous lines through to the frame, I made circles by drawing around an egg cup to provide a simple graphic pattern.

As a contrast to the dark background, I painted these curved shapes in an egg-yolk yellow to echo the tiny hints of yellow within the postcard, ensuring that the postcard and frame would go hand in hand.

This is a design trick I use regularly in my interiors. For headboards, I pick out secondary colours from within the fabric design and repeat them on the depth of the headboard's frame to create a powerful border (opposite).

# REBECCA'S PAPER PUZZLES

**There is something so uplifting about receiving a handwritten card in the post. For this project, Rebecca, in my design team, was inspired by the Victorian paper puzzles.**

Traditionally, Victorians would send these intricate cards on Valentine's Day to the lady or gentleman they were courting, but it's actually a simple yet lovely tradition to continue throughout the year. Paper puzzles involve the origami art form of folding a square of paper so that it opens not once, but twice. These puzzles fold up smaller than the palm of your hand but expand into a truly lovely surprise for the recipient. Each unfolded section can be decorated with illustrations and messages that allow the recipient to unfold to the next section.

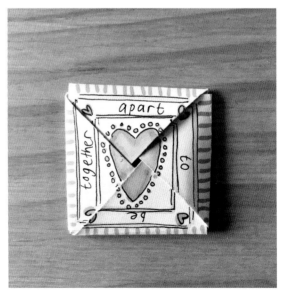

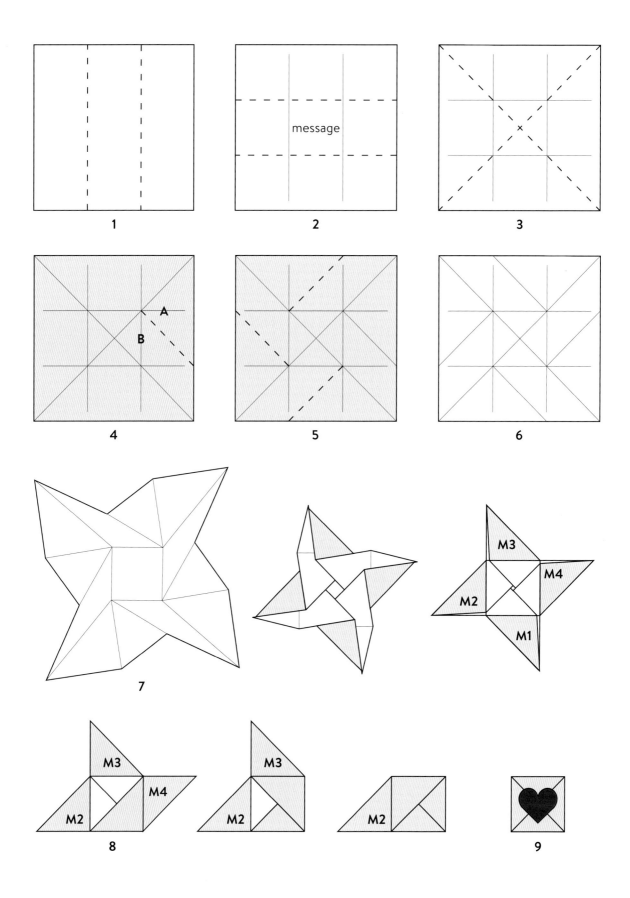

1

2

message

3

4

A
B

5

6

7

M3
M4
M2
M1

8

M3
M4
M2

M3
M2

M2

9

A paper puzzle makes a wonderful, personal gesture to send to a friend or loved one. To create your own paper puzzle, all you need is a piece of paper and some coloured pens, pencils or paint. Then follow the diagrams opposite to learn how to fold your creation.

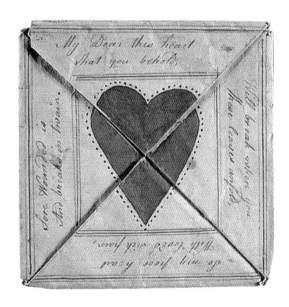

# MIMI'S SHELL MIRROR

**Handcrafted items bring energy and delight to a room – and there is nothing more charming, and reminiscent of happy, relaxing seaside holidays, than a mirror framed with seashells.**

Shellwork was a staple of 18th-century English country estates. Some of the creations were truly incredible, with entire rooms and grottos being adorned with shells. In the British seaside town of Margate, for example, they discovered a Shell Grotto in 1835 made of endless winding passages and decorated with over four million whelk, mussel and oyster shells, which were used to depict images of gods, goddesses and trees of life.

Shellwork features regularly in my interior design schemes, not only adorning mirror frames but also lamp bases, where the intricate pattern of shells turned inside out can wind up a lampstand (overleaf, bottom right), jewellery boxes and bedside tables (nightstands).

At a beach bar in Barbados (opposite and overleaf), I displayed an impressive collection of shellwork, including our version of Sailors' Valentines and old mirrors covered in shells in the most delicate tones and shapes, giving the interior a 'barefoot beachcombing' vibe.

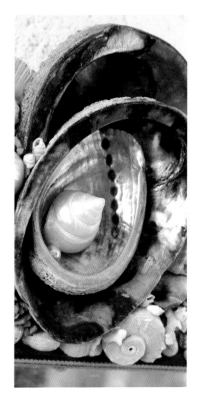

India, in my design team, has created this fun and creative way of putting shells to good use.

*What you will need:*
Mirror
Selection of shells
Old newspaper
Easy-peel masking tape
Small paintbrush
Good-quality all-purpose
  adhesive

## Step 1. Find a mirror

Ensure your mirror has either a flat frame or no frame at all – these can be found on eBay, or you might have one at home that needs a little TLC. Any shape will do.

## Step 2. Source some shells

Make sure you have shells in a variety of shapes, sizes and colours, not forgetting some smaller shells or even pebbles for the gaps. Search online or access via craft shops, but please be sure to source shells from sustainable sources, with ecological certification.

## Step 3. Protect with tape

Protect the mirror itself, which will not be decorated, with some newspaper secured with masking tape.

## Step 4. Plan the design

Lay out your design before starting. Symmetry is important because it gives your mirror a sense of order and a more designed look.

## Step 5. Add the shells

Use the paintrbrush to glue the larger shells into position first and then work your way out from there, filling in the gaps with smaller shells and pebbles. Try to cover the whole frame, mixing and matching the shells to get the desired look. Don't forget to vary the colour so your design really stands out of its own accord.

Shellwork needn't stop at mirrors. If you are decorating the outside of a little box, again remember to keep your design symmetrical. You can try using other materials too – small stones, pearls or maybe even something with a bit of sparkle, turning something ordinary into an object of beauty and individuality that you're proud to display.

# STELLA'S POTATO BLOCK

I have long been drawn to the irregularities and handmade qualities of the ancient craft of hand block printing – there is something picture-perfect in block printing's imperfections.

Traditionally, the repeat pattern for block printing is hand-carved into wooden blocks.

This is an intricate process – and really an art form in itself – that can take years to master, so for this project, Stella, in my design team, has simplified things by using potatoes instead. Accessible, affordable and ideal for making stamps for printing!

Stella decided to add a decorative border to an old tablecloth (below), but this method is great for adding detail to a leading edge of a pair of curtains or for creating your own fabric for cushions. It is also equally effective on paper for letters and cards.

*What you will need:*
Potatoes
Sharp knife
Pencil
Fabric
Acrylic paints (in colours of
  your choice)
Fabric painting medium
Paintbrush
Cotton buds

### Step 1. Choose a design
This doesn't need to be elaborate or detailed, just something simple that will look strong or interesting as a repeat. For this design, we took inspiration from a carpet detail, a carved wooden planter, and floral and foliage motifs gleaned from the garden (overleaf).

### Step 2. Create your stamps
Cut a potato in half and use the pencil to draw the design on the cut side of the potato. Cut around the design so that it stands in relief by about 5 mm (¼ in). Repeat with other potato halves until you have all the shapes you need for your design.

### Step 3. Paint the pattern
Mix each acrylic paint colour with some fabric painting medium (following the manufacturer's instructions on the bottle), then use a paintbrush to apply your first colour to one of the potato stamps and start stamping.

### Step 4. Keep stamping
Continue printing with your potato stamp. Each time you lift the stamp you will get a slightly different impression, which adds to the excitement of the process. Applying a thin layer of paint to the stamp between each print helps with consistency, but this is optional depending on how saturated you want the colour to be.

We created this Patchwork Potato design (above)to raise funds for the Charleston Trust as part of The Great Potato Printing Society with Molly Mahon.

## Step 5. Vary the effect

Apply the paint less frequently to a stamp if you want a more faded effect, as for the leaf stamp shown here (opposite, bottom left and right).

## Step 6. Add details

Use cotton buds to add extra details, in this case for the flower stalks and seeds.

The repetition is incredibly calming and the end result so satisfying. All you need is time, some potatoes and a little inspiration!

# POLLY'S PATCHWORK LAMPSHADE

Lampshades are the perfect medium for injecting personality into a living space using colour and pattern. Polly Carter, our design assistant, has been creating handmade lampshades using leftover cuttings from our many interior design projects.

Here's how to transform a plain lampshade that you would like to jazz up using recycled fabric samples:

*What you will need:*
Plain lampshade (preferably a
    drum shape)
Tape measure
Large pieces of paper
    (for the template)
Old scraps of fabric or textiles
    you love
Pinking shears
Iron and ironing board
Sewing pins (optional)
Sewing machine or a needle
    and thread
Sewing pins (optional)
Fabric glue or all-purpose
    adhesive
Clothes pegs (clothespins)

Ribbon
Pom-pom, beaded or feathery
    trim (optional)

### Step 1. Create a template
Make a paper template of the surface area of your chosen lampshade by measuring the circumference and the height. The template will be there to guide you in terms of shape and size.

### Step 2. Get creative
Cut up the scraps of fabric or textiles: use pinking shears to stop the threads in the fabrics from pulling apart. Arrange the fabrics into a fun patchwork pattern. When you are happy with the design, take a photo of the arrangement for reference.

### Step 3. Iron the textiles
Before you start sewing the fabrics together, it is important to ensure they are completely flat and straight.

### Step 4. Start sewing
Use a sewing machine to stitch all the fabrics together: start with two pieces of fabric right sides facing and sew down one edge in a straight line. It can be helpful to use pins to hold the pieces together. Then open out the two fabrics and iron the flaps on the back flat. Continue this process until all of your fabrics make up one big patchwork.

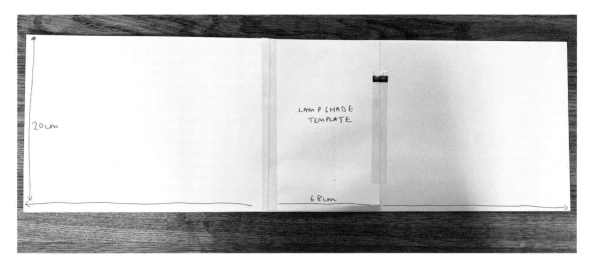

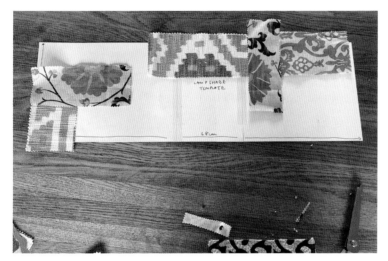

### Step 5. Iron again

Using the iron, press down on the back of the patchwork so the flaps are all flat. Turn the patchwork over and iron the front to ensure the whole piece is completely smooth.

### Step 6. Glue into place

Slowly and gently glue down the fabric, turning the lampshade as you do so. Clothes pegs can be used to keep the patchwork in place while it is drying.

### Step 7. Trim and tidy

Neatly trim away any unwanted overhanging fabric from the top and bottom of the lampshade, leaving just enough to fold over the inside lips. Conceal the jagged edge of the shade with a length of ribbon (ironed first) that works well with your pattern; you can also run the ribbon down the vertical edge of the lampshade seam.

### Step 8. Add a finishing touch

If you wish, for a final flourish, add a fun pom-pom, beaded or feathery trim around the bottom of the shade.

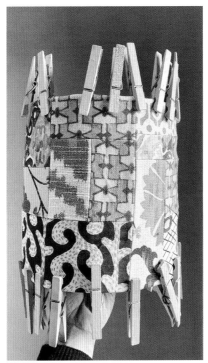

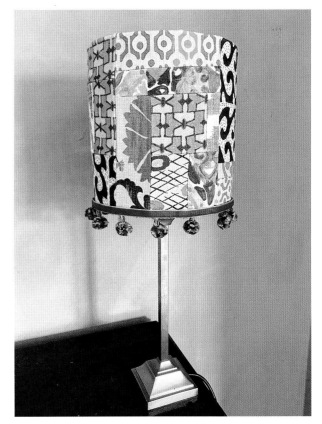

# MELISSA'S TREASURE BOX

When it comes to styling a room, I choose
pieces with their own story to tell. One such
accessory, large or small, is the treasure chest.
Every room should have one – whether used as
a larger piece that acts as a coffee table, or as a
jewellery or memento box placed on a bedside
table (nightstand).

I particularly love highly decorative boxes and chests, which conjure images of long-lost treasure, history and nostalgia. Painted chests, also known as hope chests or glory boxes, were once used to keep safe dowry gifts, such as special clothing, linens, quilts, china and silver; today, they are perfect for protecting and preserving precious trinkets, keepsakes, letters and photographs.

One of my favourite treasure boxes is this gorgeous bright green chest painted by the designer and painter Melissa White, which was included in my pop-up at Bergdorf Goodman (opposite), displayed as a little coffee table. Decorated on top with prancing unicorns, it worked perfectly as a colourful accent in the corner of the shop.

Here are some tips from Melissa White, Decorative Artist, on how to create these works of art at home:

*What you will need:*
Large wooden box or chest
Stain block (optional)
Chalk paints in different
  colours (such as Annie Sloan
  or Colourman Paints)
Paintbrushes
Art projector (optional)
Sandpaper
Furniture wax
  (clear and toluene-free)

**Step 1. Find a box**
This pine chest was found in an antique shop in Hastings, in East Sussex, England. It was a well-made box, but without any aged patina or lettering that needed to be preserved, so it was perfect for painting. You can also find antique and unique pieces on Etsy or eBay. Otherwise, any beautiful old box you might have at home will do.

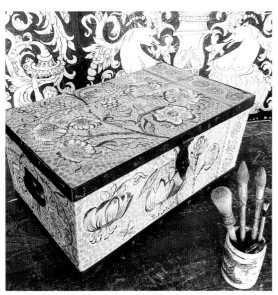

### Step 2. Find inspiration

When designing your treasure box, take creative composition and inspiration from other sources – try architectural elements, motifs from illustrations and even wallpaper as starting points. This Unicorn Box features some of the elements Kit and I included in our Andrew Martin collaboration. The panel pattern around the sides was taken from an Elizabethan wall painting at Harvard House in Stratford-upon-Avon (below).

Don't forget the inside of the chest is just as important as the outside – it's a great way to fill the box with extra details to discover (top left).

### Step 3. Use the right paints

Sometimes an old box will have been used to store oil paint or other liquids which can bleed through any paint put on top. I recommend using a stain block to prevent this, although, personally, I rather like how the history of a box can permeate, literally and metaphorically.

My boxes and chests have a chalky, aged feel to them – chalk paints used on furniture distress well since they don't contain plasticisers (binders). My favourites are by Colourman Paints and Annie Sloan. These paints work best when waxed to allow the layers of paint to come through, intimating a patina of depth and age.

### Step 4. Prepare the background

Apply an all-over base coat – here I used dark green so that it would appear through the second coat of lighter green when the paintwork was rubbed back. Paint with thick, random brushstrokes to build up texture, going back over the paint as it starts to dry to create even more texture.

### Step 5. Paint the design

Once the base coat is finished, paint the patterns and borders freehand to create a spontaneous feel. To make more detailed elements like the unicorns balanced and centred, use an art projector to guide your hand or draw these freehand if you feel confident. The unicorns are a motif we've used several times before – initial versions were inspired by an early 19th-century watercolour found in a book about American Folk Art, but each time they have evolved, a little like Chinese whispers. The shield with the maze between the two unicorns was derived from a Tudor woodblock print.

### Step 6. Paint the side panels

The pretend panelling around the sides, while intentionally wibbly-wobbly, was marked out beforehand to ensure it would fit the sections. Once you have painted the main elements of the design, stand back and assess the balance and any gaps. I couldn't resist painting a spotty border inside the lid of this box.

### Step 7. Add details

If you wish, add an accent colour as a finishing touch to excite the eye – here I painted red stripes on the mouldings to add some framing.

### Step 8. Sand and wax

Lightly rub the chest down with sandpaper to break up the paintwork, then finish the piece with a generous coat of wax. This will sink into the paint and reveal the layers of colour exposed by the sandpaper. When buffed, the chest will have a soft, mellow sheen that enhances all the brushstrokes and textures built up during the painting process.

# MINNIE'S EMBROIDERED MAGICAL MICRO GARDEN

*Above and page 239: embroidery
design by Yumiko Higuchi*

My daughter Minnie, in my design team, loves to escape into the magical world of embroidery. While it is a labour of love, it is a craft you can do anywhere – in bed, while watching TV or sitting at the kitchen table with an afternoon cup of tea.

Here she tells us about her inspirations and how to create an embroidered garden:

For inspiration, I look to the work of embroidery artists like Tokyo-based Yumiko Higuchi. I am inspired by her flawless designs and I collect her books – *A Year of Embroidery* and *Embroidered Botanicals* are

two are my favourites. To create this magical micro garden (below), I looked to the shapes and colours of tulips, daffodils and wildflowers to guide my design. I usually sketch out the embroidery pattern first before deciding which stitches I'm going to use. If this is your first attempt at embroidery, start by experimenting with running stitch and chain stitch.

*What you will need:*
Piece of fabric
Size 25 Special Embroidery Thread (Floss) in different colours
Cardboard bobbins
Embroidery hoop, 20 cm

(8 in) in diameter
Embroidery needles (ideally, French embroidery needles with sharp points; the size will depend on the amount of thread/floss you use)
Tailor's shears or sharp scissors

**Step 1. Find the fabric**
Choose a fabric you would like to embroider. Here, I used a linen fabric from The Cloth Shop in a flint colourway – it's a fabric we often use for walling in. We try to recycle most of our fabrics, so I'm lucky to have lots of wonderful linens in storage. Don't feel restricted to soft furnishing fabrics – cotton shirts can also be embellished, as can

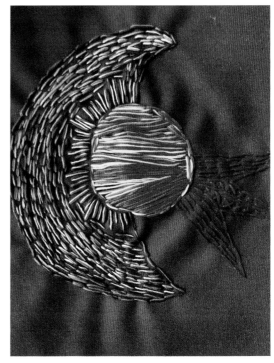

felts and wools. If you have sharp needles, you can even embellish denim jackets and pockets.

## Step 2. Wind the threads

Wind all your threads around cardboard bobbins (below left). This will make it easier to see the colours and help you create better schemes. Here, I used thread by DMC from France, which is known for its vivid colours and lustrous texture.

## Step 3. Start embroidering

Secure your piece of fabric in the embroidery hoop, ensuring it is nice and taut. You might want to sketch your design out lightly in pencil first before you start embroidering. Now start stitching.

Minnie reproduced this design (left) by stitching onto white linen. It would look wonderful framed or made into a table runner.

Another example of Minnie's embroidery is this 'La Diosa de Oro' chair (opposite), which she designed and embroidered entirely by hand. The naïve, colourful stitching brings to life the story of the female bullfighter Conchita Cintrón, who is also known as La Diosa de Oro or The Golden Goddess. Proof that anything can inspire an embroidery, limited only by your imagination.

# RUBY'S COLLAGE

The art of collage is a constant theme in my interior schemes – it's a lovely reminder that we can find beauty in just about anything, whether it be the subject matter or the materials we use.

I love the work of artist Ruby Kean, whom I've been lucky to work with as part of my design team in New York. Her framed collages, intricate and delicate, are like miniature entryways into other worlds. The collages she has made, incorporate coat tags, pieces of wallpaper, ribbon and ephemera – the one for Dorset Square Hotel is cricket-themed, while Charlotte Street Hotel's is Bloomsbury-inspired.

Here, Ruby gives some ideas for creating your own collages at home:

Collage is the process of bringing together an array of inspirations, ideas and textures to create something entirely new. By stitching a variety of materials, I can tell a layered and emotive story, sometimes quite elaborate and evocative, which is imbued with hidden meaning due to the nature of the old luggage tag or snippets of vintage textiles I might use. I think of them as visual feasts.

*What you will need:*
Card, a mixture of vintage card and paper
Glue, a special permanent adhesive double-sided tape with a polyester base (sometimes PVA for more fiddly pieces)
Scissors, H Webber tailor sheers, plus a smaller pair of embroidery scrissors for detailed snipping
Decorations like ribbons, twine, pressed flowers

### Step 1. Choose a theme
I developed these four collages around the themes of Delight, Fortitude, Passion and Victory (opposite).

### Step 2. Organise your materials
I find joy in gathering together things that might otherwise have been discarded or dismissed. Teared sheets from old magazines, train or theatre tickets and scraps of vintage passementerie are all a constant source of inspiration.

### Step 3. Add embellishments
Once you've laid your overall look, add further texture with layers of different hand-crafted papers, pressed flowers, fabrics and ribbons, to create depth and interest.

# APPLIQUÉ AT HOME

Adding handcrafted touches, such as appliqué and needlepoint, helps to further extend the narrative design of an interior. These details are always a wonderful reminder of the hand of the person who created the stitches in a cushion, for example, or carved the curves of a table leg.

I am always creating new appliqué designs to have hand-stitched onto cushions, the backs of chairs and headboards.

In the Brumus Bar & Restaurant at Haymarket Hotel (above), named after one of my beloved dogs, my design team hand-cut and appliquéd different breeds of dogs onto the back of each chair and barstool in his honour.

# Customise your chairs at home

In this lovely bedroom at Covent Garden Hotel, we appliquéd a bold snail shape onto smart boiled wool to create these whimsical bed cushions (above).

In a bedroom at Crosby Street Hotel, in New York, I created a graphic orange motif, inspired by an orange tree fabric used on the headboard, and carried it through from the bed cushions to the upholstery of an armchair (opposite).

For my 'Folkthread' collection for Anthropologie, I created upholstered armchairs, with appliqué flying rhinos and a dashing jungle cat for hand-stitched cushions to embody my love of folk art and handmade crafts (above left and right).

# It doesn't need to be perfect, that is part of the charm

# APPLIQUÉ CUSHION

**This appliquéd bed cushion (above) sits on the bed of Room 109 at Dorset Square Hotel.**

This friendly little creature has been cut out from dark blue boiled wool and fixed to the cushion fabric using invisible stitching. He stands proudly with a strong red crown on his head. Jewels are embedded in the crown using a yellow thread and little French knots. Yellow cut-out moon shapes give the scene a dream-like quality.

*What you will need:*
Plain cushion cover
Felt or wool (these won't fray like linen or cotton)
Embroidery thread (floss) and a needle
Cotton sewing thread and a needle
Scissors

### Step 1. Find inspiration

For this cushion I was inspired by flicking through David Yarrow's dramatic black and white photography of large cats. Once you have found something you like, trace over it and tweak it until you have a design you are happy with.

### Step 2. Scale and cut around the shape

Once you have drawn out your character, you may need to scale it up to the size you think will work for your cushion. Then transfer your shape onto the felt or wool and cut it out.

### Step 3. Choose your colours

The room that this cushion was designed for had a red, blue and white scheme. I carried this colour palette through to the cushion, giving our 'catty creature' a little red crown.

### Step 4. Get stitching

This design was made with four different threads – yellow, red, white and blue – using simple yet effective markings to show a mane, feet and bushy tail. The yellow thread was used for French knots to create jewels in the crown, while red thread was used to stitch down the yellow felt moons.

### Step 5. Fix it down

Once you are happy with your work, fix your friendly creature to the cushion. We used invisible stitching by colour matching a cotton thread to our navy wool, fixing the design to the light grey boiled wool chosen as the base cloth for the cushion.

# CRISTINA'S CANDLESTICKS

**Hand-painted candlestick holders provide another way for injecting joy and personality into any space.**

I have always had an affection for playful candlesticks, from the kitsch to the more traditional (opposite) – they can dress up any fireplace or dining table, even without the wick burning.

For this pair of candlesticks (below right), my team were inspired by one of the handmade fabrics used in a suite Soho Hotel, which harks back to the ancient technique of appliqué used in Central and Southern Asia, and particularly northern India (see page 251).

To create something similar for your home, all you need is some acrylic paints, untreated wooden candlesticks (which can be sourced online) and an idea for patterns or motifs that will complement the mood of your home, whether echoing the colours in a favourite textile or the geometric lines of an architectural chair.

We designed
these candlesticks
to bring a hint
of whimsy to the
dining table

Last year, I collaborated with the talented ceramic artist, Andrea Kashaniour, to create candlestick holders inspired by my fabric collection 'Mythical Creatures'. Together, we worked hard to get the colours just right. They have been modelled in a soft and fluid way, a far cry from the more austere and restrained tradition of candlesticks. These designs are a witty and quirky addition to any home (opposite).

# ABOUT KIT KEMP

**Kit Kemp MBE** has forged an internationally-acclaimed reputation for not only her unique interiors as co-owner and Creative Director of Firmdale Hotels and Kit Kemp Design Studio but also as an author and successful textiles, fragrance and homewares designer. She is a highly-respected champion of British art, craft and sculpture. Kit is the creative force behind Ham Yard Hotel,  The Soho Hotel, Covent Garden Hotel, Charlotte Street Hotel, Haymarket Hotel, Number Sixteen, Knightsbridge Hotel and Dorset Square Hotel in London and Crosby Street Hotel and The Whitby Hotel in New York. Her work spans from concept to completion of projects both inside and out. It ranges from restoring historic buildings to creating newbuild hotels, often injecting energy and life into surrounding neglected areas. Kit has collaborated with leading global design brands including Chelsea Textiles, Christopher Farr, Andrew Martin, Fine Cell Work, Wedgwood,  Wilton Carpets, Anthropologie, Porta Romana and Annie Selke creating collections which span tableware to furniture, fabric and wallpaper. This is her fourth book. Other books by Kit Kemp are: *A Living Space, Every Room Tells a Story and Design Thread.*

# THANK YOU

2020 has been a challenging year but I have been amazed by the creativity and adaptability of my team in the Kit Kemp Design Studio. Thank you for all your diligence and sense of fun and fabulousness. Thank you to the craftsmen and artists, artisans and builders, and the curtain, furniture, rug and frame makers who make it all appear easy. Thank you Firmdale team, in particular the wonderful Craig Markham, Annabel Cliff and Madeleine Phillips. Kate Pollard and Kajal Mistry at Hardie Grant; photographer Simon Brown; and designer David Eldridge for making every page look inviting. Fiona McCarthy for making sense of the text and S.J. Axelby for creating such beautiful opener illustrations. Thank you Tim, Tiffany, Willow and Min for your constant love and inspiration.

# EXPLORING COLOUR

## # KITKEMPDESIGNTHREAD

Illustrations by Olivia Thompson

Published in 2021 by Hardie Grant Books, an imprint of Hardie Grant Publishing

Hardie Grant Books (London)
5th & 6th Floors
52–54 Southwark Street
London SE1 1UN

Hardie Grant Books (Melbourne)
Building 1, 658 Church Street
Richmond, Victoria 3121

hardiegrantbooks.com

British Library Cataloguing-in-Publication Data. A catalogue record for this book is available from
the British Library.

Design Secrets by Kit Kemp
ISBN: 9781784884246

10 9 8 7 6 5 4 3 2

Publisher: Kajal Mistry
Art Direction: David Eldridge
Photographer: Simon Brown
Copy Editor and Captions: Fiona McCarthy
Editor: Caroline West
Illustrations: SJ Axelby and Olivia Thompson
Production Controller: Katie Jarvis
Colour Reproduction by p2d
Printed and bound in China by Leo Paper Products Ltd.

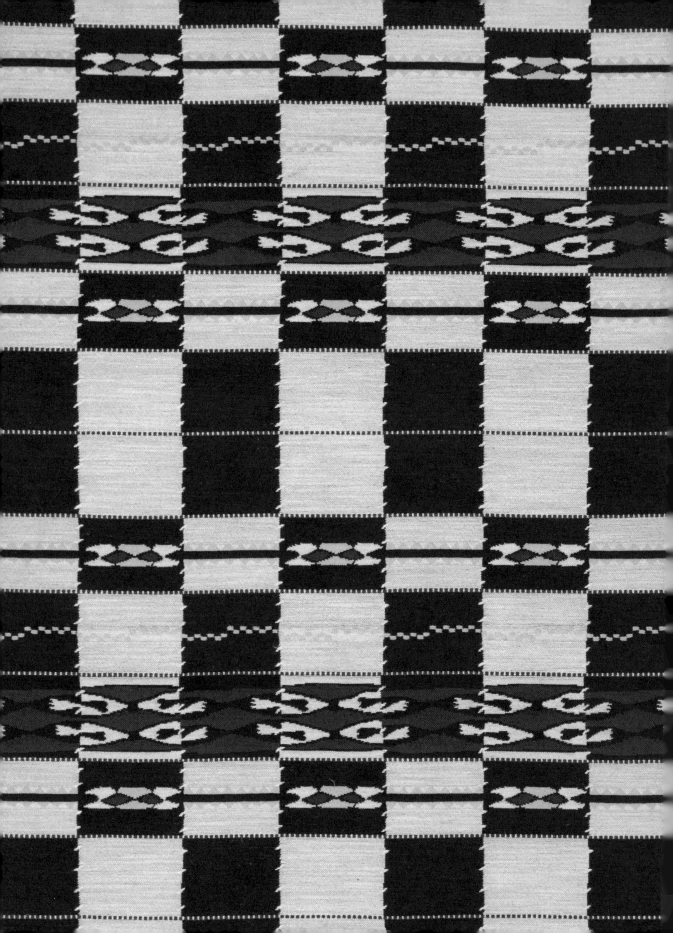